Media & PUBLIC LIFE

Media & PUBLIC LIFE

Edited by

EVERETTE E. DENNIS
&
ROBERT W. SNYDER

Transaction Publishers
New Brunswick (U.S.A) and London (U.K.)

Library of Congress Catalog Number: 96–17934
ISBN: 1–56000–874–1
Printed in the United States of America

Library of Congress Cataloging-in-Publication Data

Media and public life / edited by Everette E. Dennis and Robert W. Snyder.
        p.   cm.
    Originally published as vol 9. no. 1 of Media studies journal, Winter 1995.
        Includes bibliographical references and index.
        ISBN 1–56000–874–1 (paper : alk. paper)
        1. Mass Media—United States.   2. Mass Media—Social aspects—United States.   I. Dennis, Everette E.   II. Snyder, Robert W., 1955–   .
P92.U5M39   1996
302.23'0973—dc20   96–17934

Contents

Preface   xi

Introduction   xiii

Part I Media and Public Life

1. Journalism as an Act of Education   3
   Jonathan Alter, Albert Gore Jr. and William A. Henry III
If journalism is to educate, then journalists need an honest definition of
fairness, an appreciation of the future and a commitment to the real interests
of the public.

2. How Vast the Wasteland Now?   5
   Newton N. Minow
In 1961 the author, then chairman of the Federal Communications Commission,
called television "a vast wasteland." Thirty years later, he urges a new
generation "to put the vision back into television, to travel from the wasteland
to the promised land and to make television a saving radiance in the sky."

3. Traits of a Good Reporter   11
   Thomas Winship
Advice from a veteran editor, distilled from his own career and the careers he
has observed, for aspiring journalists and those who will hire them. "First
look for a high energy level."

4. In the South—When It Mattered to Be an Editor   13
   Dudley Clendinen
The civil rights movement challenged Southern newspaper editors to take a
stand on racial equality, writes an author and journalist with personal and
professional roots in the South. "Those who had the courage and integrity to
claim the moment, who saw the right and spoke for it, were few in number,
but they filled a tremendous void created by politicians who were less clear-
eyed and forthright."

5. Seething in Silence—News in Black and White   23
   Ellis Cose
"For reporters, race can be a treacherous subject, raising questions that go to the heart of the journalist's craft," observes the author, a contributing editor at *Newsweek*. "Anyone doubting the polarizing potential of race in America (and beyond) need look no farther than the typical American newsroom."

6. Surviving Being a Survivor, Or, Whatever Became of
   What's Her Name?   33
   Betsy Wade
One of seven named plaintiffs in the landmark 1973 sex discrimination suit *Boylan v. Times*, who today writes the *New York Times*' "The Practical Traveler" column, recalls the fight against inequality and the lessons learned therein. "Though we may walk invisible among our legatees, we know that we opened doors for a new generation that may not know they were ever closed."

7. Requiem for the Boys on the Bus   43
   Maureen Dowd
A woman who has covered national political campaigns turns the tables: It's not the appearance of women journalists that tamed the boys on the bus. "Before the new breed of New Age stiffs came on the campaign bus in the last few years, things were different," writes the author, a White House reporter for the *New York Times*. "Now the road is filled with a bunch of 30-something, touchy-feely guys, tying up all the cellular phone circuits trying to call home to talk baby talk to their wives and kids."

8. The Best Seat in the House?   47
   Lawrence K. Grossman
"History will measure our nation's achievements not by our wealth or our superiority in our free-market forces, but by our cultural legacy and the character of our civilization." The author, a former president of the Public Broadcasting Service, and now president of the PBS Horizons Cable Network, shows how the arts got lost in the commercial imperatives of television.

9. From Pollock to Mapplethorpe—The Media and the Artworld   59
   Arthur C. Danto
A scholar and critic explores the role of the media in transforming art from a private matter to a subject for public debate. The author concludes, "Art has come a long way and society has come a long way, with the media the mirror of their mingling."

10. A Decade of Change   69
    Compiled by Jennifer Kelley
Results of Media Studies Center dialogue and *Media Studies Journal* interviews
on critical trends and events in the media with comments from Ken Auletta,
Walter Cronkite, Jannette L. Dates, Alex Jones and Robert Schulman.

Part II The Media, Politics and Policy

11. Journalism, Publicity and the Lost Art of Argument   77
    Christopher Lasch
"What democracy requires is public debate, not information," argues a cultural
historian. "Increasingly information is generated by those who wish to promote
something or someone—a product, a cause, a political candidate or
officeholder—without arguing their case on its merits or explicitly advertising
it as self-interested material either. Much of the press, in its eagerness to
inform the public, has become a conduit for the equivalent of junk mail."

12. Bystanders as Opinion Makers—A Bottoms-Up Perspective   87
    Herbert J. Gans
"The conventional wisdom about public opinion has it shaped largely by
opinion makers—by the politicians and other persuaders," writes a Columbia
University sociologist and media scholar. "Nonetheless, the prime controllers
of long-term public opinion, the people who dispose over it and propose more
of it than the conventional wisdom gives them credit for, are the Americans I
call bystanders. These are the normally politically uninvolved members of the
general public, and altogether they constitute the vast majority of that public."

13. Let's Put on a Convention   95
    Reuven Frank
A former president of NBC News, who created the standard for modern
television convention coverage, explains why the networks have cut back on
live convention coverage. "There is, in sum, no more news at conventions."

14. A Consumer's Guide to Media Truth   103
    Patricia O'Brien
"Most of us are media consumers, and we all—media people and 'civilians'
alike—have a big stake in figuring out what's objective and fair in the news
and what isn't." Here is a 10-point plan from a journalist, novelist and former
presidential campaign press secretary.

15. The End of Predictability   105
     James F. Hoge Jr.
"The Cold War was a simple measuring stick for determining the relevance and importance of international affairs," writes a former newspaper editor-publisher and currently editor of *Foreign Affairs*. "With the old gauges broken, the press is struggling to understand the new international order of risks and opportunities."

16. Follow That Tank!   113
     Bernard Kalb
A veteran foreign correspondent reflects on how new technology reduces the autonomy of correspondents and speeds the transmission of news. "Has all the speed made for better reporting?"

17. The Flickering Images That May Drive Presidents   115
     Robert MacNeil
"Television has created a different order of public opinion," writes the former executive editor of the "MacNeil/Lehrer NewsHour." "In the issues that touch foreign affairs, the public witnesses the same apparent reality as its leaders. The public is no longer a mass to be sold a policy after it is decided. It is now active in seeing policy made and, one might even say, getting policy made."

Part III What Kind of Future?

18. Peering Over the Edge   125
     Ken Auletta
Changes in economics and ownership have transformed the television networks and their place in American society. A media analyst and author analyzes the causes, the consequences and the prospects for the future. "The networks need to find a way out of their trap, which is that they rely on a single source of revenue and are but three channels in a 150-channel universe."

19. Media Complexes and Juvenile Distractions   135
     Vitaly Korotich
Much of American media is "burdened by complexes and juvenile distractions that are not really indicative of American life," observes a Boston University professor who once edited a Moscow newsweekly. Nevertheless, CNN and the *International Herald Tribune* "have become prototypes for tomorrow's mass media, uniting us in humanity."

20. Media Globalism in the Age of Consumer Sovereignty   137
   Anthony Smith
It is a paradox, argues the president of Oxford's Magdalen College: While a substantial number of the world's entertainment businesses are concentrated into huge international companies, media technology has made it easier and cheaper for new firms in all media to enter the market. "What we need to understand are all of the cultural implications of the rapidly changing media map of the world."

21. The Inevitable Global Conversation   151
   Walter B. Wriston
Government efforts to regulate the revolution in communications are either wrong or ineffectual, argues the former CEO of Citicorp. "Fortunately for us all, the market has a way of supplying what people need or want if the government gets out of the way, or sometimes even if it doesn't."

22. Highway to the Stars or Road to Nowhere?   159
   Leo Bogart
An author and media scholar explores the possible consequences of new information systems. "The pioneers of television had the sense that they were riding the crest of a great wave of changes that went far beyond communication to engulf every aspect of human life. The architects of today's telecommunications deals and mergers are no less conscious of the changes they are fashioning. Do they have the same sense of responsibility and concern for the consequences?"

23. Prospects for the Future   173
   Compiled by Jennifer Kelley
Results of dialogue and interviews on trends to watch for in the future with comments from Leo Bogart, John Corry, Walter Cronkite, Jannette L. Dates, Neal Gabler, George Gerbner, Loren Ghiglione, Suzanne Braun Levine, Newton N. Minow and Craig L. LaMay, Anthony Smith and Tabitha Soren.

For Further Reading   183
Index   185

Preface

Just what role the media plays in public life—whether they are seminal agenda setters or transmission belts for others—has occupied commentators and critics, scholars and journalists for decades, if not centuries. It is a debate that traverses much territory involving the power of the media and their interaction with individuals, institutions and society.

Media and Public Life is an effort to explore and examine many of the propositions that probe the relative impact and influence (or in some instances, lack of it) of the media in America and the world. What is presented here is drawn from more than a decade of work that appeared mostly in the *Media Studies Journal* (formerly the *Gannett Center Journal*) between 1985 and 1996. Originally presented as a souvenir for the *Journal*'s parent, the Media Studies Center's tenth anniversary in 1995, the issue sold out on newsstands and was frequently requested by people in newsrooms and classrooms in the United States and abroad, as well as by citizens from many venues. This book, organized from "the best of the *Journal*," captures much of the controversy and debate that engaged the media industries and their various constituents in the public over a seminal decade marked by convergence of technologies, greater concentration of ownership, the end of the Cold War and a turbulent journalistic debate over the future of news.

As the founding executive director of the Media Studies Center and founder also of its *Journal,* I had the privilege of stewardship of a unique nexus between the media, the academy and other institutional interests for nearly 12 years. During all of that time we strove to be more than an elitist enclave, a media monastery, but a useful resource for the citizens everywhere. We did that in the *Journal,* which was offered for sale on newsstands nationwide, through public conferences, much media comment and books like this one. I believe that this volume represents the best of the work that appears in some 33 issues of the *Media Studies Journal,* 95 books by Center fellows and some two dozen by staff and other associates. This volume encompasses much of the substance and spirit of that work.

Now from the vantage point of a new assignment involving a strategic alliance of universities related to media studies, I am pleased to present this collection of articles and essays, all of which offer explanations on the role and operations of media and media industries as they interact with the lives of people everywhere.

Everette E. Dennis
Executive Director,
International Consortium of Universities,
The Freedom Forum
Arlington, Virginia

Introduction

For over a decade the institution which gave voice to the ideas contained in this book analyzed the media, joined in debate about the media and proposed solutions to problems that divide the media and the public. Recognizing that change in the field of communication can move either instantly with the dispatch of news or glacially with the structure of institutions, we've often been satisfied if those efforts lead to better professional, scholarly and public understanding.

We've watched the world change with the end of the Cold War and the rise of democracies and market economies almost everywhere—conditions that have generally, although not always, benefited freedom of expression. At the same time, and virtually everywhere in the world, we see trends toward globalism and bigness that are particularly apparent in the concentration of media enterprises. This has happened concurrently with and to some extent because of technology and the loosening of governmental regulations and controls. "The structure is the message," some critics posit and generally we agree. The frameworks and forces that guide and oversee the communication industry also have a deep impact on the messages it produces.

In this retrospective volume, first assembled in 1995 at The Freedom Forum Media Studies Center of Columbia University, we've tried to reflect the spirit of 10 years of published work, to sample some of our strongest and most lasting essays while regretting that space makes it impossible to include many influential articles, commentaries and interviews. From its beginning the *Media Studies Journal* encouraged a range of reports, studies and essays. Each isssue has been organized around a single topic, but the writers in each issue have rarely agreed with each other. We tried to reflect the range and diversity of the growing field of communication and media studies, encouraging some of the most gifted writers and thinkers of our time to enter the fray.

We've considered the great functions of communication (like information, opinion, entertainment and publicity) as well as trends (like news in the post-Cold War period) and specific industries (like radio and book publishing). The importance of content has never been far from our line of sight. Our work has included the pacesetting "Race for Content" issue and other issues covering key topics such as race, the environment, schools and higher education. Because our mandate at Columbia is the advanced study of "mass communication and technological change," we've also taken up technology topics, as we did in our issue "Media Wars."

Through all of our work we have emphasized the consequences and impact of media institutions on society and public life. Similarly, we have mapped the territory of current controversies and long-term trends to factor out the people and the forces at issue. We've identified problems and tried either to understand them or solve them in the context of institutional history, the current state of affairs and probable futures.

In *Media and Public Life,* the 10-year retrospective presented here, we've tried to define a decade of inquiry on the media and lay out questions for the future. In addition to time-tested pieces, some of which have been edited and reshaped for reasons of space, this book includes the results of a panel of leading commentators, media professionals and scholars who kindly spent time assessing important developments of the last 10 years, issues for the next decade and even influential works worth reading.

In 1995, on the occasion of the 10th anniversary of The Freedom Forum Media Studies Center, we saluted many individuals who contributed to our work, much of it reflected over the years in the pages of the *Media Studies Journal.* Although the *Journal* is slightly younger than the Center, media professionals, critics, scholars and other citizens began to develop material for this publication almost as soon as we opened our doors. Indeed, several of the articles and shorter commentaries that appeared in the opening issues of the *Journal* had their genesis in the early work of fellows and staff members at the Center as well as our National Advisory Committee, associates and other friends and colleagues.

Organizing a retrospective volume like this one recalls our original prospectus for the *Journal* developed by staff and debated vigorously in our National Advisory Committee. It also suggests our appreciation for those who have played major roles in shaping and editing the *Journal* along the way, notably Huntington Williams III, Craig L.

LaMay and Edward C. Pease, all of whom have moved on to other assignments. Importantly, Jane D. Coleman, former associate director of the Media Studies Center, was part of the creation of the *Journal* and the Center's early research programs. Additionally, assistant editor Lisa DeLisle and former senior editorial assistant Barry Langford, a part of the *Journal* staff for all of its history till 1994, deserve special recognition.

As we selected the material for this book and made agonizing choices about what to include and exclude, we were drawn once again to an article by Richard C. Wald, senior vice president of ABC News, which appeared in our inaugural issue. What he said then resonates well today and bears re-examination. As he wrote in "A Ride on the Truth Machine":

> The mass-ness of America's mass media has developed in roughly the same span of time as Americans have lived under the Constitution, and the progress from Colonial printer to billion-dollar media corporation has gone, like the country itself, in fits and starts. Mass media have been governed by the law of Unintended Consequences, driven by wars and inventors, and always subject to imperatives of commerce and public policy.
>
> Steering a course bounded by the private interest that draws people to the journalistic enterprise and the public interest that makes it worthwhile, the American news industry came from beginnings that were acceptable, but not really as respectable as the people in it like to think. And after a long and raucous development, the news business has arrived at a kind of establishment-blessed state of grace that seems permanent, but probably is not.
>
> We are the children of fathers whom we barely recognize. We have grown into a respectability, a self-regard, that may strangle us. The forms in which we ply our trade, like the matter we deal in, are forever changing—and not necessarily for the better.

We believe that the spirit of informed inquiry that Mr. Wald invoked to help launch this publication is equally valid today. Moreover, it is a guide for the exploration and understanding of developments yet to come. We invite you to consider the questions and answers raised here. The answers that you find are a useful agenda for any citizen who cares about public life and the media today.

Everette E. Dennis
Robert W. Snyder

I

Media and Public Life

1

Journalism as an Act of Education

Jonathan Alter, Albert Gore Jr. and William A. Henry III

JONATHAN ALTER: Just as rigid political attitudes are the enemy of good media criticism, a rigid view of media fairness is the enemy of good journalism. The most popular misconception in American journalism today is probably the confusion between point of view and unfairness. If a journalist has a point of view, it often seems, he or she can't be doing the job right. Journalists who pretend to an objectivity they can never fulfill, or who are unwilling to end up out of step with the public opinion, can contribute to this misconception.

Good journalism has to have an edge.

—Jonathan Alter is a senior editor at Newsweek. *His comment is excerpted from "The Cloak of Fairness," which appeared in the winter 1988* Media Studies Journal, *"Regulating the Media."*

ALBERT GORE JR.: The media have a responsibility to inform and to educate, to tell us not only what is happening, but also why it is happening and what it will mean to us—today and tomorrow. They can and should not only report what is happening, but what could happen—cover not only the millions who gather to celebrate Earth Day, but also the stories we'd never see if not for their efforts—reports of thinning of the upper atmosphere, acid rain killing far-away forests. In every arena the media lead and prod policy-makers. Editorial writers and columnists, television and radio commentators and talk shows impact policy and perception. News reporting, by drawing attention to problems and issues, moves policy. Environmental reporting is no different.

—Vice President Albert Gore's comment is excerpted from "Steering by the Stars," which appeared in the summer 1990 Media Studies Journal, *"Covering the Environment."*

WILLIAM A. HENRY III: In an ideal world, politics itself is, like journalism, a form of education, and one of the principal aims of a political campaign is to educate voters so that they are better able to decide for themselves where they stand on the issues and how they can best see their beliefs carried out. In the real world, of course, a great deal of politics too often turns out to be about getting elected, taking power, then rewarding the people who helped get you there. Similarly, a great deal of journalism turns out to be self-absorbed, and the invocation of the First Amendment is frequently of the press, by the press, for the press, without much reference to the genuine interests of the public.

—William A. Henry III, who died in 1994, was a senior writer and book reviewer at Time. *His comment is excerpted from "Liberty and the News: Walter Lippmann Revisited," which appeared in the spring 1987* Media Studies Journal, *"The Business of News."*

2

How Vast the Wasteland Now?

Newton N. Minow

The phrase has become so famous that it overshadows its own context: Everybody remembers the "vast wasteland"—the words with which Newton Minow, President Kennedy's young appointee as FCC chairman, branded commercial television before the National Association of Broadcasters on May 9, 1961. But fewer are aware that Minow's administration led to a thoroughgoing reassessment of the debt American television owed to the "public interest"—a process that led ultimately to the establishment of the Public Broadcasting Service.

So on May 9, 1991—the 30th anniversary of his famous broadside—The Freedom Forum Media Studies Center invited Minow to Columbia University to deliver a progress report on American television. How has broadcasting served the American people over the intervening decades? Can it ever assume the role of cultural leadership that would validate its ubiquitous presence? And will there arise another New Frontier, heir to the hopes of 30 years ago, to challenge the wasteland in the millennium?

In that speech, I asked the nation's television broadcasters "to sit down in front of your television set when your station goes on the air and stay there without a book, magazine, newspaper, profit-and-loss sheet or rating book to distract you—and keep your eyes glued to that set until the station signs off. I can assure you that you will observe a vast wasteland. . . .

"Is there one person in this room who claims that broadcasting can't do better?. . . Your trust accounting with your beneficiaries is overdue."

Today that 1961 speech is remembered for two words—but not the two I intended to be remembered. The words we tried to advance were "public interest." To me, the public interest meant, and still means, that we should constantly ask: What can television do for our country?—for the common good?—for the American people?

Alexis de Tocqueville observed in 1835: "No sooner do you set foot on American soil than you find yourself in a sort of tumult. . . . all around you everything is on the move." What would Tocqueville have said about the explosive expansion of telecommunications —particularly the electronic media—during the 30 years between 1961 and 1991?

Choice has skyrocketed. The VCR means you can watch a program when you want to see it, not just when the broadcaster puts it on the schedule. If you are a sports fan, a news junkie, a stock market follower, a rock music devotee, a person who speaks Spanish, a nostalgic old-movie buff, a congressional-hearing observer, a weather watcher— you now have your own choice. The FCC objective in the early '60s to expand choice has been fulfilled—beyond all expectations.

Yet, to many of us, this enlarged choice is not enough to satisfy the public interest. There are several reasons. Although some viewers have gone from a vast emptiness to a vast fullness, others have been excluded. Choice through cable comes at a price not all can afford, and cable is still not available to the entire nation. And as CBS President Howard Stringer said in a speech at the Royal Institution in London last year, "We see a vast media-jaded audience that wanders restlessly from one channel to another in search of that endangered species— originality. . . . more choices may not necessarily mean better choices."

Can this be changed where television is concerned? My own answer is yes. If we want to, we can provide the American people with a full choice, even if the marketplace does not meet the demands of the public interest. I reject the view of an FCC chairman in the early '80s who said that "a television set is merely a toaster with pictures." I reject this ideological view that the marketplace will regulate itself and that the television marketplace will give us perfection. The absolute free market approach to public good has been gospel in our country in the case of the savings and loan industry, the airline industry, the junk bond financing industry, and in many other spheres of commerce and common interest. If television is to change, the men and women in television will have to make it a leading institution in American life rather than merely a reactive mirror of the lowest common denominator in the marketplace. Based on the last 30 years, the record gives the television marketplace an A+ for technology, but only a C for using that technology to serve human and humane goals.

In the last 30 years, the television marketplace has become a severely distorting influence in at least four important public areas. We have failed 1) to use television for education; 2) to use television for children; 3) to finance public television properly; and 4) to use television properly in political campaigns.

In these four areas, the television marketplace has not fulfilled our needs and will not do so in the next 30 years. These four needs can be met only if we—as a nation—make the decision that to aim only at the bottom line is to aim too low. If we still believe in the concept of the public interest, we can use television to educate, we can stop short-changing our children, we can fund public broadcasting properly, and we can provide free television time for our political candidates. My generation began these tasks, and the time has now come to pass the responsibility on to the next generation—the first generation to grow up with television.

What will happen in television from now until 2021? In the next 30 years, four main forces—globalization, optical fiber, computers and satellite technology will illuminate the crossroads.

Well before 2021, I believe there will be convergence of the technologies now used in telephones, computers, publishing, satellites, cable, movie studios and television networks. Already we see tests of optical fiber demonstrating the future. We see 400- and 500-channel systems on the horizon, fragmenting viewership into smaller and smaller niches, and we need to remember that for all their presumed benefits these developments undermine the simultaneous, shared national experiences that comprise the nation's social glue.

As this new technological world unfolds, the risk remains that we will create information overload without information substance or analysis, of more media with fewer messages, of tiny sound bites without large thoughts, of concentrating on pictures of dead bodies instead of thinking human beings.

When we launched the first communications satellite in 1962, we knew it was important—but we had little understanding of its future use. I did tell President Kennedy that the communications satellite was more important than launching a man into space, because the satellite launched an idea, and ideas last longer than human beings. The last 30 years have taught us that satellites have no respect for political boundaries. Satellites cannot be stopped by Berlin Walls, by tanks in Tiananmen Square or by dictators in Baghdad. In Manila, Warsaw and Bucharest, we saw the television station become today's Electronic Bastille.

Before he was elected president, John F. Kennedy once compared broadcasters and politicians in these words: "Will Gresham's law operate in the broadcasting and political worlds, wherein the bad inevitably drives out the good? Will the politician's desire for re-election—and the broadcaster's desire for ratings—cause both to flatter every public whim and prejudice—to seek the lowest common denominator of appeal—to put public opinion at all times ahead of the public interest? For myself, I reject that view of politics, and I urge you to reject that view of broadcasting."

The '60s started with high hopes, confronted tragedy and ended in disillusion. Tragically, our leaders—President John F. Kennedy, Reverend Martin Luther King Jr. and Pope John XXIII—left too soon. We cannot go back in history, but the new generation can draw upon the great creative energy of that era, on its sense of national kinship and purpose, and on its passion and compassion. These qualities have not left us—we have left them, and it is time to return.

As we return, I commend some extraordinary words to the new generation. E.B. White sat in a darkened room in 1938 to see the beginning of television—an experimental electronic box that projected images into the room. Once he saw it, Mr. White wrote: "We shall stand or fall by television—of that I am sure. . . . I believe television is going to be the test of the modern world, and that in this new opportunity to see beyond the range of our vision, we shall discover either a new and unbearable disturbance to the general peace, or a saving radiance in the sky."

That radiance falls unevenly today. It is still a dim light in education. It has not fulfilled its potential for children. It has neglected the needs of public television. And in the electoral process it has cast a dark shadow.

A new generation now has the chance to put the vision back into television, to travel from the wasteland to the promised land, and to make television a saving radiance in the sky.

Newton N. Minow, a former FCC chairman, is an attorney and former director of the Annenberg Washington Program in Communications Policy Studies of Northwestern University. This chapter originally appeared in a longer form in the fall 1991 Media Studies Journal, *"Media at the Millenium."*

3

Traits of a Good Reporter

Thomas Winship

First, look for a high energy level. It's all too easy for a reporter to ease into slack habits because of the "down" time built into the ebb and flow of news. Would that every reporter was hungry to get his name in the paper. (A medic who developed an energy meter would make a killing.) Next, look for signs of innate curiosity about everything—people, social relations, things familiar and unfamiliar. What goes with this, of course, is the chutzpah to satisfy that curiosity. Shrinking violets need not apply. Finally, look for the ability to write clearly and gracefully. Most reporters either have it or they don't. This can easily be measured, through clippings, college writing and tests under deadline.

Satisfy yourself on these three characteristics before signing on each hire, and the chances are pretty good you might come up with an acceptable 50 percent success record.

I confess to several other hiring prejudices. I am partial to 1) the unorthodox, off-beat type, 2) reporters and editors fresh out of college, 3) veterans, with previous wire service or alternative press experience, 4) adventuresome travelers, 5) omnivorous readers, 6) women—because they work harder and are more sensitive, 7) people who have not moved too quickly from one city to another, 8) self-educated reporters and editors, 9) people with a sense of humor, and 10) Yalies over Harvards. They write better.

Find an applicant with a third of these attributes and you're lucky.

Thomas Winship is the former editor of the Boston Globe *and currently chairman of the International Center for Journalists. His comments are excerpted from "Genes, Romance, and Nepotism (and Other Essential Qualifications for the Journalist),"* which originally appeared in the spring 1988 Media Studies Journal, *"The Making of Journalists."*

4

In the South—When It Mattered to Be an Editor

Dudley Clendinen

I grew up in Tampa, a small Gulf port city that considered itself Southern, in a neighborhood of new frame houses whose young family occupants had migrated out of smaller towns and cities, out of the Depression and through World War II, and into the shallow waters of a tide of growth and change that was just beginning to flood the South, lifting it from its ancient cultural moorings.

It was 1948 when we moved to that house from my parents' war-time apartment, and our neighbors were a sample of the emergent South. Among the husbands were an eye doctor, an airport manager, a trial lawyer, a truck salesman, a realtor, a furniture store owner, a lumberyard manager, two insurance brokers—and my father, a newspaper editor.

Some of the men in our neighborhood had been raised in cities like Tampa or Birmingham, but a number had come out of the hamlets and farmlands in north Florida, Mississippi, Alabama and South Carolina.

Two or three had no college education, but most had been to the state university and most had finished. A few had the benefit of family money, but many were the first university graduates in their families in some time, and almost all of them had been taken up by the military and sent out of the South, for training if not for war. Theirs was a transition generation. They were, in fact, the last white generation in American history to grow to adulthood in a South still ruled by old caste law, still cloaked in its old myths and habits of mind; and in them, in the generation, indeed in that neighborhood, were all the elements of the white South accustomed to its past but also conditioned and equipped by change for a different future.

They were on the hinge, and so were the editors of the newspapers they read. Born into a system that conferred nobility on whites at birth, they were destined to experience the events that elevated blacks to full citizenship and reduced whites to mere people after all. It all began to happen as they raised their children after the war: Segregation began to fall, and black civil rights were fought for and imposed by laws.

The enormous process that was the postwar South would have run its course no matter how the neighbors in Tampa or Selma or Jackson or Little Rock reacted or what their newspapers told them. But it was a period unlike any other in that the basic cultural distinctions by which people lived began to change forever. For white Southerners, that generally meant without their instigation or consent. They needed information to help them understand what was going on and why they should not be violently opposed. They needed sharp-minded arguments that would shred the mythology in which the South and its racial system had long been cloaked. They needed wise men at a time when frank truth and wise perspective were in desperately short supply.

It was also a time whose circumstances favored newspapers and whose people needed them. When my family moved to the new neighborhood in Tampa in the summer of 1948, President Truman had just ordered the armed forces desegregated. The process thus began. No house yet had a television, but almost every home had a black maid, or shared one. And every house got the morning paper. John N. Popham, the first Southern correspondent named by the *New York Times*, had just begun to cover the region. "Just as soon as Truman made that decision in 1948, the Southern governors had their first meeting in

Wakulla Springs, Florida," Popham recalls. "From then on, it was a racial story."

The news columns of Southern papers weren't very curious or deep or original in the late 1940s and 1950s. They followed sports and politics actively enough, but the whole rational thrust of Southern culture from the time of John C. Calhoun on had been self-defensive and maintaining. It had to be, to justify the unjustifiable in a society dedicated first to slavery and then to segregation and subservience. Tradition was everything, and the news pages were simply not in the habit of examining the traditions of the South. Popham himself was from an old Virginia family whose world of kin, college and military connections stretched across the entire region. "A lot of rank and file reporters in those days were racists, you know. If you got out to Mississippi," he says, "you were lucky in those days to find two people who weren't."

The news pages, in fact, were destined to grow sharper in the heat and competition of covering the civil rights movement itself, just as Vietnam later taught journalists to be more critical of the government's conduct of foreign policy. The reporters and news editors learned lessons from Popham's coverage in the *Times*, and from Claude Sitton, who followed him as Southern correspondent, and from John Herbers, Roy Reed and Eugene Roberts, who followed Sitton in the job. They were Southerners all in the days when the *Times* was the only American newspaper that gave the South a full-time correspondent.

Popham invented the form and emphasis of Southern coverage, criss-crossing the South like a honeybee, drawing his sources together in a web of information and exchange: white racist governors but also white political scientists and university administrators, new institutions like the Southern Regional Council and previously unheard black voices in civil rights organizations, pulpits and colleges. Popham was close to Ralph McGill in Atlanta. He spent time with Hodding Carter in Greenville, Miss. He came to Tampa and talked to all the newspaper editors who watched the region. As the 1950s unfolded, Popham's network became a way and a means by which others, the non-Southern reporters who began to pour into the South, could learn how to understand it.

Across the South in neighborhoods like ours, literate whites were accustomed to looking to their newspapers' editorial pages to tell them what to think about things. They looked to the editorial pages for local, state and Southern perspective, and to news weeklies like *Time* and *U.S. News and World Report* to understand America and its place in the world. The mind of an editorial page editor could roam freely over terrain and through issues that were off-limits to reporters. The reputations of many Southern papers, in fact, were largely shaped by the individual prose, personality and point of view of their editorial page editors, who sometimes simply bore the title of "editor." In a region absorbed by mythology and history and politics, a region that loved anecdote, rhetoric and personal flourish, this editorial page focus was an honored tradition. But for many publishers it was also a cheaper and safer tradition than committing the news resources of the paper to a real examination of the culture. Newspapers like the *Atlanta Constitution*, owned after 1950 by the Cox family of Ohio, were notoriously cheap.

"If you sent somebody to Little Rock or you sent somebody to Selma, you had to explain yourself," said Eugene C. Patterson, who, as the first executive editor of the *Atlanta Constitution*, was in charge of the news staff. (Patterson succeeded Ralph McGill as the editor in 1960 and won the Pulitzer Prize for editorial writing in 1967.) "But even publishers were accustomed to sighing and turning the page when it came to editorials."

Thus for 20 years or more, while the region tortured itself over the issue of race, the white newspaper editors of the South—the writing editors—had a role, a forum and an authority unequaled before or since. Those who had the courage and integrity to claim the moment, who saw the right and spoke for it, were few in number, but they filled a tremendous void created by politicians who were less clear-eyed and forthright.

Romance about the past has been the South's addiction, but we should not wax romantic about the unclouded vision and unbiased sense of social justice evidenced by the Southern editors who rose to the occasion. They weren't Solomons. They weren't detached. They weren't omniscient. And they weren't in charge. They didn't all believe in integration, not personally or immediately and certainly not at first, and they couldn't always see clearly all the ramifications of right and wrong in whatever piece of the issue was before them at the moment. They couldn't always write all of what they could see either, for fear of getting so far ahead of their readers that they would lose credibility. As Taylor Branch reminds us in *Parting the Waters*, when

President Truman submitted a civil rights package to Congress in 1948 asking for a federal anti-lynching law and other measures, Ralph McGill condemned the legislation in the *Atlanta Constitution* as being too radical for the South.

But if ever there was a time when Southern editorialists achieved a prominence, an influence and a distinctive voice heard throughout American journalism and public affairs, it was in the years from World War II until 1970. That was a time when it mattered to be a writing editor, if the editor chose to matter, because to be born white in the South then was to inherit either a sense of privilege or the realization of moral crisis, just by accident of place of birth. Few people got beyond the satisfaction of privilege, but editors had to keep a cultural watch. Whether they accepted the evil nature of the inherited system or not, they knew its imbalance and reacted to its excesses out of love and pain for the region and its people, and out of an outraged sense of decency.

Senator Eastland, speaking to a meeting of the White Citizens Council in Mississippi in 1955, had declared that the integration ordered by the U.S. Supreme Court threatened "the racial integrity, the culture, the creative genius and the advanced civilization of the white race." In making the *Brown v. Board of Education* decision, he said (as quoted by Stephen A. Smith in *Myth, Media and the Southern Mind*, University of Arkansas Press), the court had been responding to "a radical pro-Communist movement in this country." Senators, governors and elected officials in other Southern states spoke in similar idiom, and when a North Carolina high school and a Jewish temple in Atlanta were bombed in the fall of 1958, Ralph McGill wrote in his daily front-page column:

> Let us face the facts. This is the harvest. It is the crop of things sown. It is the harvest of defiance of courts and the encouragement of citizens to defy law on the part of many Southern politicians.

When Gov. Ross Barnett of Mississippi joined the front rank of those politicians in the fall of 1962, vowing to keep applicant James Meredith and all other blacks out of the University of Mississippi forever, Ira Harkey, the editor and publisher of the 7,000-circulation Pascagoula daily, condemned him as a demagogue leading the state to disaster. One man in a county of 54,000 people came to his support. Harkey faced gunshots, falling circulation and threatened advertisers.

A cross was ignited on his lawn. Non-Southerners, he mused in an editorial, cannot "understand the full terror of a cross burning, this classic threat from the Klan. It is like the voice of doom, the sentence of death, the placing of the victim beyond the pale." But Harkey was not frightened off. On Christmas 1962 he wrote this:

> In Mississippi, a person who attempts to carry Christianity out the church door, who dares to practice the Christian virtue of tolerance outside the church, is cursed as a liberal, a leftist, a communist, a niggerlover. Christ was the greatest champion of the underdog the world has ever known. If He were to visit us here, now, by whose side would He stand, beside the brick-throwing, foulmouthed, destroying, profaning, slavering members of the mob and their 'nice-folk' eggers-on, or beside the trembling victim of their hate?

A white woman employed in the local library who read the editorial wrote to Harkey, "Instead of a bullet through your door, I hope you get a bullet through your stupid head." Friendless, emotionally spent and separated from his wife, he sold out the paper that he had built from a weekly and left the state the year after he won the Pulitzer. Harkey went on to earn a master's and doctoral degrees, to write two books and teach at several universities. He did not return to Mississippi.

The owners of small-town papers could write what they wanted to write. They owned the presses. But the ones with the moral courage to criticize the culture in which they lived and did business did so at the peril of their lives and livelihood. "Every one of them that I knew was scared pissless while they were doing it," says Hodding Carter III. "It has always defined bravery for me."

The Pulitzer board understood that. One of its members during the 1950s was Carter's father, the editor of the *Delta Democrat-Times* in Greenville, Miss. When the senior Hodding Carter was honored in 1946 for a group of editorials on a subject of racial, religious and economic intolerance in Mississippi, he was the first Southern editor to win that prize in almost 20 years. But in the wake of the *Brown v. Board of Education* decision, the board awarded the whole run of Pulitzers, beginning with Buford Boone's prize in 1957, to editors in the South. Eleven of the 15 awards for editorial writing from 1946 to 1971 went to Southern editors, and the issue that fired 10 of them was race. Only one recipient, Hazel Brannon Smith, owner and editor of the *Lexington Advertiser*, was a woman, but none was any braver. She had fought the back-shooting segregationist sheriffs and other dark lights of the Delta for 10 years before she won the prize in 1964. She endured personal ostracism, bombing and economic boycott until her husband's career and her own finances were ruined, until the unrepaired roof over her press fell in, until she ran out of money and finally lost her mind to old age.

Like the men in my boyhood neighborhood, virtually all the men who won Pulitzers for their editorials had seen military or government service in the war and had attended or graduated from some university. One experience or the other had taken them out of the South. Except for John R. Harrison and John S. Knight, all were native Southerners, but in each case that birthright had been leavened by experience. Hodding Carter Jr., the first contemporary Southern editorial winner, had gone to college in Maine, worked for *Stars and Stripes* in North Africa and been a Nieman fellow at Harvard. And so it went. Even Ralph McGill, a member of an earlier generation, had his eyes opened by a year of travel in Europe on a Julius Rosenwald Fund fellowship just before World War II. "Travel, war and education made a difference," Gene Patterson said. "Getting out of the South was awfully important. You couldn't help but come back with some questions."

Horace G. ("Buddy") Davis Jr., a native Georgian, Army Air Corps veteran and University of Florida journalism professor who won the prize for the *Gainesville* (Fla.) *Sun* in 1971 while writing free-lance editorials at the rate of about $15 apiece, was the last Southerner to be honored for writing honestly and compassionately about race relations in that period of intense focus on the South and its racial turmoil. By then, the major civil rights legislation was several years old, and the nation's conscience was mired in Vietnam. But that does not mean that race has ceased to be a subject, or that it has become easy to tell the South the truth about itself. The columns for which Claude Sitton, editor of the *Raleigh* (N.C.) *News and Observer*, won the Pulitzer Prize for commentary in 1983 dealt in part with civil rights issues and with the South's most notable current demagogue, Sen. Jesse Helms. And Albert Scardino, who won the Pulitzer Prize in 1984 for his editorial in the *Georgia* (Savannah) *Gazette*, touched issues that the city's papers of record would not touch, but Scardino could not attract the business support they enjoyed. The editorially distinguished *Gazette* failed financially. Scardino and his wife Marjorie closed it in 1985 and moved to New York. He now writes for the *New York Times*, and she is an editor for *The Economist*.

In fact, the region to which the South's great editorial writers once belonged is no longer oppressively and peculiarly in the South. Race is still an issue—as the *Atlanta Journal and Constitution* has demonstrated in the last two years, by winning one Pulitzer and nominations for two others for reporting how white social, political and economic systems still take advantage of blacks. Moral questions still abound. And the Southern establishment still does not appreciate hard truths. But the basic change is this: to live in the South is no longer to live in a state of moral crisis.

I don't mean that Southern editors matter little now. A whole range of regional issues are in need of editorial comment and illumination now and in the future. They tend to be "sunbelt" issues. The region has become homogenized. And the ownership of its newspapers and the ranks of its editors are more homogenized too. The Southern voice has been blended out.

The character of the South and its cast of people have both changed. That is the march of history. It may be that the most symbolic piece of architecture in that regard is the John Seigenthaler editorial straddle. Seigenthaler was perhaps the most personally involved and in some ways the most courageous activist-editor of the civil rights era. For decades he symbolized the editorial personality and liberal philosophy of *The* (Nashville) *Tennessean*. He continues as the publisher of that paper. But after Gannett acquired it, he also became the editorial director of *USA Today*.

Tread, tread, the march of history. It may be that the South today, a place with no consuming moral crises, needs no known familiar voice of conscience at the paper to thunder and implore and spiral to lyrical heights of moral suasion. "It isn't necessary to have that sort of person at the paper today," says John N. Popham, who served as managing editor of the *Chattanooga Times* after leaving the *New York Times*. "The total paper has to amount to something."

In other words, the quality of the whole record must be good in order for a community and a region to have a chance of knowing themselves and how they relate to the nation and to the world. That is essentially the approach that Nelson Poynter and then Eugene Patterson and now Andrew Barnes took and take as chairmen of the *St. Petersburg* (Fla.) *Times*, and that is the approach Bill Kovach took when he resigned as Washington editor of the *New York Times* to become editor of the *Atlanta Journal and Constitution* 30 months ago.

It has been the dream of Southern journalists to have a great and central paper in the South, a paper committed to the quality of its whole record and not simply to the sound of its voice and the depth of its coin. Ralph McGill, in his greatest stature as editor and then as publisher, was never allowed to realize that dream. And for all the energy and vision invested by men like Kovach and other journalists now departed or still in Atlanta, it is a dream that remains elusive and may now in fact be dead. The new editor of the *Atlanta Journal and Constitution*, Ron Martin, was chosen from *USA Today*, where this declaration of purpose appears on the masthead: "*USA Today* hopes to serve as a forum for better understanding and unity and to help make the USA truly one nation." Devoid of political or emotional content, that stands not so much as an editorial philosophy as a statement of homogenization as a marketing strategy.

Another masthead is close at hand, from the *St. Louis* (Mo.) *Post-Dispatch* in September 1963, on the Thursday after four black children were killed when white racists bombed the church in Birmingham. It was a day and an era when the South knew shame and white editors wrote in anguish from the philosophical and emotional depths of their souls. The *Post-Dispatch* had reprinted Eugene Patterson's column from the *Constitution* and, from the *Tampa* (Fla.) *Tribune*, an editorial by James A. Clendinen, my father. The words of both editorials ring like bells today, but on the masthead above them, timeless and astonishing in their commitment, float the words of Joseph Pulitzer, whose awards brought honor and support to Southern editors who needed honor when they were needed in their time:

Never tolerate injustice or corruption, always fight demagogues of all parties, never belong to any party, always oppose privileged classes and public plunderers, never lack sympathy with the poor, always remain devoted to the public welfare, never be satisfied with merely printing news.

Dudley Clendinen is a former national correspondent for the New York Times. *He is now writing a history of the modern gay rights movement with Adam Nagourney. This chapter originally appeared in a longer form in the spring 1989* Media Studies Journal, *"The Opinion Makers."*

5

Seething in Silence—News in Black and White

Ellis Cose

For reporters, race can be a treacherous subject, raising questions that go to the heart of the journalist's craft. Is objectivity (or even fairness) possible when dealing with people from different racial groups and cultural backgrounds? Can any of us be trusted to make sense of lives essentially alien to our own? Does "getting it right" mean anything more virtuous than conforming to prevailing prejudice?

Journalists are inclined to believe that a good eye and an unbiased heart can ensure essential accuracy, regardless of the personal (or racial) baggage one brings to the table. Yet as Ben Bagdikian notes in his classic *The Media Monopoly*, "News, like all human observations, is not truly objective. . . . Human scenes described by different individuals are seen with differences." Arguably, no differences loom larger than those connected with ethnicity and race.

Anyone doubting the polarizing potential of race in America (and beyond) need look no farther than the typical American newsroom. Last year, in attempting to assess the impact of race on American lives, the *Akron* (Ohio) *Beacon Journal* also took a look at itself. With nine white and eight black journalists, the paper formed two separate focus groups. What it quickly discovered was that although all of the participants worked at the same institution, they saw it quite differently. The blacks, by and large, believed that the deck was stacked against them. Despite the fact that the publisher was an African American, many felt that the real control resided in the hands of whites who understood neither them nor their community.

In contrast, the white journalists at the *Beacon Journal* felt that blacks (and black issues) were receiving special treatment. As the paper's 1994 Pulitzer Prize-winning report observed, whites at the paper felt a "constant pressure . . . to bend over backward to embrace minority perspectives." Indeed, anxiety among whites seemed even higher than among blacks. And practically everyone—regardless of race—seemed fearful of speaking their minds. Whites feared being censured as politically incorrect; blacks fretted over repercussions that might affect their careers if they dared to complain about racism.

Responses of focus groups comprised of ordinary citizens were strikingly similar to those of the journalists. The *Beacon Journal* found that while blacks saw racism as a constant in their lives, whites felt that racism (especially institutional racism) had largely been eliminated. The paper also discovered that people had a hard time talking honestly about race, and everyone—regardless of race—seemed troubled and frustrated by the pressures that race questions imposed on their lives. As the *Beacon Journal* report put it, "Whites are tired of hearing about it. Blacks wish it would go away. All seem powerless to move it." The paper went on to observe, "The typical white American will go to great lengths simply to avoid the subject. And that skittishness may be getting in the way of solutions."

Journalists, of course, are supposed to be different from ordinary citizens, at least when it comes to confronting difficult truths. But race, it seems, can make cowards of us all. It is not merely cowardice, however, that makes honest racial dialogue difficult. The difficulty also derives from the fact that perceptions vary radically as a function of race—or, more accurately, as a function of the very different experiences members of various racial groups have endured.

In the past two years (since the massive riots in Los Angeles), a number of major newspapers have produced impressive in-depth reports on race relations in America. The narratives are uniformly somber and, in some respects, dispiriting. The *Chicago Sun-Times* focused on what it called the "great divide," and presented an extensive poll documenting just how wide that divide has become. The *Indianapolis Star*, sounding a similar theme, quoted a local minister who said, "There are no race relations. We are two different communities in two different worlds that hardly have anything to do with each other."

In its seven-month series, the *Times-Picayune* of New Orleans traced American (and its own city's) race relations from slavery to modern times and concluded with a forceful and sober editorial:

> We live separately. Worship separately. We stand apart, frozen that way by the mythical but overpowering thing called race, America's arbitrary, color-coded system of defining, dividing and oppressing. It is a painful fact, so much so that we can scarcely talk about it. But we must.
>
> During the past seven months, the *Times-Picayune* has tried to do that with its series "Together Apart: The Myth of Race." We have done so with the abiding belief that our quality of life and the very future of our community depend on that dialogue.... Through two years of research, hundreds of interviews, dozens of stories and pictures and thousands of callers' comments, this newspaper has tried to show that any meaningful solution we might propose ... must begin with a simple, yet monumental conversation.

The editorial went on to observe and confess: "It's a queasy undertaking, talking about race. Especially when your own house is not in order." Indeed, as the *Times-Picayune* worked through the questions raised by the series, it found its own staff to be a microcosm of the divisions it detailed in greater New Orleans. In order to help it resolve the difficult internal issues, the newspaper brought in outside "diversity" experts to work intensively with its newsroom staff. Sig Gissler, a Freedom Forum Media Studies Center senior fellow who examined the *Times-Picayune* case, likens the process to an organization going into exhaustive group psychotherapy.

Few news organizations are prepared to go to the trouble and expense of putting their staffs on the equivalent of a psychiatrist's couch. Yet, without some artificial form of intervention, America's newsrooms seem destined to remain divided along racial lines.

In an attempt to explore life across those lines, the *Indianapolis Star* sent several black and white reporters into places or situations where persons of their race were not normally found. Some reporters went on interracial "dates." Some visited each other's homes, an experience that led one white reporter, Bill Theobald, to admit, "My views about race have mostly been formed by thinking, by reading or by talking to whites. Talking to blacks about the subject is uncomfortable. I don't know how to ask the questions; perhaps I am afraid of the answers."

Such soul-searching was doubtlessly healthy for the *Star*, but the fact that it took a newspaper series to get veteran journalists to emerge from their cocoons is not exactly reassuring. Yet Theobald's relative racial isolation appears to be the norm in the news business, and that isolation goes a long way toward explaining why the perspectives of black and white journalists are often very far apart.

The National Association of Black Journalists' 1993 *Muted Voices* study was in large measure a testimonial to the existence of that perceptual gap. The survey of NABJ members and white managers found that the two groups see the world from such different vantage points that it is difficult to believe they work in the same industry, much less in the same newsrooms. Seventy-three percent of the NABJ members polled thought blacks were less likely than other journalists to advance; only 2 percent of the white managers felt that way. Most of the black journalists surveyed thought blacks were forced to spend more time than whites in entry-level positions. Only 2 percent of the managers thought so. Question after question yielded similar results, and although the NABJ survey compared white management to black staffers, it's a good bet that much the same would have been found if the researchers had polled whites and blacks of more equal status.

A 1991 Ohio University job-satisfaction survey found that white journalists, by and large, believed that whites were at a significant disadvantage in newsrooms. Two-thirds of the white respondents thought minorities received preferential treatment, and one-third believed that minorities received more opportunities than whites.

"At the present time, my newspaper discriminates on the basis of race and sex," one respondent wrote. "White males need not apply or expect to be treated the same as others in the newsroom."

As the poll clearly documents, the sense of disadvantage among white journalists is widespread, even as minority journalists continue to complain that they are the ones discriminated against—though these complaints, typically, are not voiced aloud. The NABJ survey found, for instance, that one-third of the black respondents were afraid to raise racial issues out of fear that to do so would damage their careers.

A decade ago, management consultant Edward W. Jones conducted a massive three-year research project looking at blacks in corporate America and published the results in a 1986 article in the *Harvard Business Review*. Like NABJ's pollsters, Jones found an overwhelming sense among blacks that life, for them, was grossly unfair: 98 percent said that subtle prejudice pervaded their companies, and 90 percent reported a "climate of support" worse than that for their white peers. Eighty-four percent said that their race had worked to their disadvantage when it came to ratings, pay, assignments, recognition, appraisals and promotion. Fewer than 10 percent reported an atmosphere at work in which open discussion of racial issues was promoted. Conversely, when Jones talked to white management at the firms, he found that whites saw a markedly different picture: Indeed, they saw their firms as bastions of tolerance, places that were essentially color-blind.

Jones threw his hands up at the perceptual discrepancies, concluding that regardless of whose perceptions were correct "by some impossible objective standard," the corporations had a serious problem. When I spoke with him in 1992 while conducting research for my book *The Rage of a Privileged Class*, he had concluded that the workplace race situation was worse than ever: Blacks in corporations were not only still suffering but "some of us are losing hope," he said. "The psychological casualty rate is very high."

It's impossible to calculate the magnitude of any "psychological casualty rate." What is obvious, however, is that muting expression carries a price, not only psychologically but journalistically. Moreover, as management consultant Jones says, "How the heck do we solve something we can't talk about?"

Yet, if the results of the myriad focus groups, surveys and private testimony that have been conducted on this issue are to be believed, journalists are fearful of honesty. The image of journalists as reticent, fearful communicators doesn't easily square with the stereotype of loudmouthed reporters unafraid of saying whatever pops into their head. Yet, if neither white nor black journalists feel comfortable talking about race, it's unlikely that preconceptions will be seriously questioned in the press, and it's inevitable that racial coverage will be driven largely by timorousness or hackneyed tradition.

In this age of political correctness, complaints of timid coverage are not difficult to find, whether it's white journalists griping about having to cater to minorities in Akron, or conservatives accusing the *New York Times* of being overly respectful of gays. Yet, even if we assume the complaints are valid, the conventional approach to racial coverage is not a satisfactory alternative. For conventional coverage, as a number of researchers have shown, tends to disparage minorities.

Robert Entman of Northwestern University, for instance, notes that a disproportionate share of TV news and reality-based programming depicts minorities in stereotypical ways. Large numbers of African Americans and Latinos, he says, are cast as victims or victimizers of society, but few (in contrast to whites) are pictured as productive citizens.

The preponderance of such images, argues Entman, may have serious effects. For, in a country that remains largely segregated, whites' notions of what it means to be black and Latino are derived largely from what they see on television. And the picture they get, claims Entman, is of an inner city "dominated by dangerous and irresponsible minorities." In his analysis of coverage in the Chicago area, Entman found that white victims of crime were given more airtime than black victims; yet black assailants were given more extensive coverage than their numbers merited. The result, says Entman, is a picture of a society "in which minorities, especially blacks and to a lesser extent Latinos, play a heavy role in causing violence but make little contribution toward helping society cope with it."

Looking over Entman's research took me back to my days as a young writer and reporter for the *Chicago Sun-Times*. Late one Saturday night I was in the newsroom when word of a murder came from the reporter at police headquarters. Upon hearing the sketchy details, the man who was working the city desk slot hollered back to the rewrite man taking the reporter's call, "Is it a good address?"

No one in the newsroom had to ask what that question meant. We all understood that a good address was one that was affluent and white—perhaps on Chicago's Gold Coast, or in one of its ritzier suburbs. It went without saying that a tragedy in such a community was worth more ink than a tragedy in one that was not white and not wealthy. I don't recall the answer to the slot man's question, but the question itself has haunted me for some 20 years, for it sums up an essential part of conventional journalism's point of view.

Today, though we live in a world (as we constantly remind ourselves) that is increasingly multicultural, much of conventional journalism remains fixated on the lives of the white and the wealthy. I was reminded of that earlier this year, when my issue of *New York* magazine arrived. It featured an article that purported to identify the best places to find any number of products and services one might search for in New York City. I was struck by the fact that in a city that is a virtual United Nations—it is said that more than 119 languages and dialects are spoken in New York—practically every face attached to the magazine's recommendations was white. Clearly, New York, as viewed by the magazine's editors, remains a very white place.

The alternative to such one-sided coverage need not necessarily amount to twisting the news into a politically correct caricature of reality. But achieving better and more balanced journalism ultimately depends on having journalists who are wise enough and varied enough to see the world in its true complexity. Certainly, the news world is closer to that ideal than it was in, say, 1978. That was the year when the American Society of Newspaper Editors pledged that the industry's newsroom demographics would mirror the country's by the end of the century.

Every year since then, ASNE has compiled statistics that show slow progress toward that goal (albeit, not enough progress to provide much hope that it will be reached). Most recently, the percentage of minority journalists in U.S. newspaper newsrooms was computed at 10.49. (The U.S. population is approaching 25 percent minority.) At certain large papers, the percentage is considerably higher: Just over 17 percent of the newsroom work force at newspapers of over 500,000 daily circulation are members of minority groups, as were 24 percent of all first-time journalist hires and 39 percent of newsroom interns over the last year.

That some segments of the newspaper industry take the diversity effort seriously is apparent not only from the new hiring statistics but from the high-profile involvement of the Newspaper Association of America. In January 1992, the American Newspaper Publishers Association (now the Newspaper Association of America) brought together the heads of several of the nation's biggest newspaper companies. Summit conveners named a host of committees to work on various aspects of diversity. They also embraced (and broadened) ASNE's hiring goals, encouraging newspapers to achieve "work force parity with respect to women and minorities within their markets, including all levels of management, by the year 2000 or sooner."

As with ASNE, however, NAA has been plagued by questions about the seriousness of its quest and about the odds of success. At a second summit meeting in December of 1992, James Batten, chairman of Knight-Ridder Inc., grappled with those questions. "I think we all understand that NAA is not in a position to compel anybody to do anything," he said. "Our power, to the degree that we have power, comes from our ability to experiment, our ability to persuade. It comes from our ability to encourage, to educate, with maybe a touch of inspiration here and there."

It was probably as good an answer as he could have given. For the fact is that, for all the activity around the summits, NAA and the other industry organizations don't have the final word. What ultimately happens in newsrooms across America has much less to do with what NAA (or any trade organization) says than with what a myriad of individual editors and publishers decide. Setting industry goals is primarily an exercise in symbolism. This is not to say that taking such a stand doesn't have an impact. It does. Among other things, it serves to legitimize the goal of newsroom integration. And, though newspapers are far from seeing the goals achieved, they are farther along that route than the other major players in the news business. Television, outside major urban areas, is not a particularly integrated enterprise. And mainstream magazine staffs remain, for the most part, overwhelmingly white.

Yet, for all the attention annually focused on ASNE's numbers and other industry statistics tracking progress, news organizations must ultimately be judged less on the composition of their staffs than on the composition of their front pages and broadcasts. Clearly, a direct relationship exists between staffing and the news reported, but to concentrate only on hiring statistics is to lose sight of the larger issues. For even if newspapers can manage to achieve demographic parity with the general population, that alone will not guarantee a more honest and representative brand of reporting. The problem lies as much in our attitudes as in our statistics.

As the *Muted Voices* study and the *Akron Beacon Journal*'s report make clear, attitudes in the newsroom are much like those in the world we cover. To some extent, that will always be the case. For journalists cannot afford to cut themselves off from their surroundings. Yet, neither can they afford to allow racial anxieties to take precedence over honest, effective communication. For if we remain ignorant of how to ask questions or afraid of the answers those questions might provoke, we will also remain inadequate to the task of covering the news.

Ellis Cose is a contributing editor at Newsweek *and author of* The Press, A Nation of Strangers *and* The Rage of the Privileged Class. *This chapter originally appeared in the summer 1994* Media Studies Journal, *"Race—America's Rawest Nerve."*

6

Surviving Being a Survivor, Or, Whatever Became of What's Her Name?

Betsy Wade

It's a small and diminishing club I belong to: women who put themselves on the line as lead plaintiffs in the media sex-discrimination suits of the 1970s and then stayed on with the same employers. By virtue of my payroll name, I was alphabetically the first of the named plaintiffs at the *New York Times* and thus became the eponym of *Boylan v. Times*. The next to youngest of the seven, I still work there.

What happened to those of us who stayed on? Well, neither the extreme of seeing scales fall from management's eyes nor a purgatory of corporate revenge. Rather, we have been able to continue with Freud's two necessities for the whole life—love and work. Work still has its rewards, although it can no longer be seen as a climb up a career ladder; the ability to love, enriched by our intense period of organizing, sustains us more.

We remain proud. Though we may walk invisible among our legatees, we know that we opened doors for a new generation that may not know they were ever closed.

I got a sharp reminder the other day that I myself once belonged to a generation that neglected the admonition Alice Duer Miller gave about her woman's college: Do not ever take it for granted; people whose names you will never know broke their hearts to get it for you.

My reminder came because the Washington Press Club Foundation, in its valiant underfinanced task of creating an oral history of women in journalism, came to me to talk about our suit. Sitting in my kitchen with the interviewer, Mary Marshall Clark, I was recalling my 1956 farewell training from the printers at the Newspaper Enterprise Association syndicate, where I then worked. They were eager for me to excel when I went to the intimidating composing room of the *Times* as (I have been told) the first woman to do makeup. Describing my lonely struggles in a hostile hierarchy at the *Times*, I recalled only a sole woman Linotype operator—the already venerable daughter of a printer—who proudly came by to greet me but, by union protocol, from the printers' side of the stone.

The movie in my head was so clear that previously unremembered detail filled in like floodwaters. I looked at Mary Marshall in horror. "There was a woman next to me on my side of the stone," I said. "Louise Polk Huger made up the letters to the editor every day. She was there before me, pointing her pencil at the type and telling the makeup what she wanted. My God, I wiped her out!"

When I went to work for the *Times* in 1956 I was 27. Miss Huger appeared to me then to be 150, although she proved to be 53. She wore teachers' dark wool dresses, with narrow matching belts and Enna Jettick shoes, and she had a figure a lot like my ninth-grade English teacher's. I saw her but did not identify with her. But Miss Huger was rearing a son by herself, and Huger was her own name, not her husband's, and if you etched a template for a courageous pioneer, she would slide into it with no gaps.

How arrogant that I should recall young Miss Wade trotting into that blocklong composing room with her proofs, perky as Miss Piggy, bringing the fight for equality to the heartland of the International Typographical Union. Miss Huger had joined that battle well before me, although she may have seen it as a better job for herself rather than as a victory for women. A college graduate, she went to the paper in 1927, before I was born, and worked her way into editing and makeup from the stenographers' pool via a job as secretary to the publisher, a chasm not often leaped. She prevailed, not because printers thought she was a respectable motherly woman, but because she was strong. Nancy Finn, now assistant to the *Times'* chairman, recalls Miss Huger: "She was not somebody who could be pushed around."

Which is a way of explaining that when I stand in the *Times* elevator in my New Balance running shoes, anonymous and ignored by the perky women who have come to the *Times* since 1978, when *Boylan v. Times* was settled, I can claim no right to be angry, hurt or hostile. I am 150 years old and shaped like a ninth-grade English teacher. These young women know that they all made it on their own, and I hear them assert that these discrimination problems have been resolved. We knew what we did could benefit only those who followed, but we have become as invisible as Miss Huger.

Title VII class-action discrimination cases had their heyday in the '70s because of the conspicuous nature of the discrimination when we began our push (not one woman was a photographer at the *Times*, not one an art director!) and the availability of federal money for lawyers; such suits were nearly dead thereafter because of the narrowing of civil rights law in this area.

Boylan v. Times was at first financed by money distributed by the Equal Employment Opportunity Commission to encourage law schools to train lawyers for the employment law field. Harriet Rabb, a dean at the Columbia University Law School, devised the Employment Rights Clinic as a teaching-research seminar and received some of this aid.

Our preliminary steps at the *Times* came in 1972, when a few of us met over lunch to talk over a suit at *Newsweek* and where we were, which was no place. We finally drew up a bill of particulars, pressing for an affirmative action program because we had uncovered that the *Times* had a contract to sell copies to PXs, making it a big enough federal contractor to require one. We soon found our way to Rabb, baring our souls to law students from successive classes through the mid-'70s, often in the back room at Gough's saloon on 43rd Street. In the summer, Rabb hired students to do such time-consuming discovery tasks as combing a roomful of filing cabinets for sexist interview memos, of which there were many.

By the time of the settlement in 1978, the federal money was long used up. Rabb said then that the law school clinic got less than 50 cents on the dollar from its bills for the legal work she and the others on the faculty team did. Other cases, notably against the Associated Press, were undertaken by *pro bono* feminist law organizations and women's law firms, including Janice Goodman's in New York. The Newspaper Guild of New York provided money for *Rosario v. Times*, the black caucus suit that ran parallel to *Boylan v. Times*. (Benilda Rosario, the leader of one class and a notable member of the other, is also still at work, a double survivor.) The *Reader's Digest* case was handled by Rabb's clinic, which also worked on a second settlement of the *Newsweek* case. And so on down: *Newsday*, NBC and others. None ever went to trial.

These federal and *pro bono* wells have run dry, and today employees who are the victims of discrimination, most certainly in the paycheck, cannot afford to buy this quality of legal help.

Further, as case law has evolved, it is no longer possible to certify a vast, vague suing class such as "all women employed by a paper and all women turned away by the paper within a certain period." Now each member of the class must stand up and make a claim, so it is equally no longer possible for most members of an employee group to hover under the water like an iceberg while a few carry on a visible fight.

A result is that getting a class together today is harder. One sort of suit that continues is the age-discrimination suit filed by people who have been bought out, fired or refused promotions. A group of workers who lost their jobs when the phone company cut back in New York did get together in the late '80s, but their lawyer said that he weeded members out of the class when their cases looked weak. In 1991, when the *Times* bought out a big number of employees covered by the Newspaper Guild union contract—including my fellow plaintiffs Joan Cook, Grace Glueck and Andy Skinner—the paper required that all sign an agreement not to sue on the basis of age discrimination.

There never were many of us. Each case had a small number of plaintiffs who expected to be principal witnesses as representatives of all the affected employees. At the *Times* we had seven of these named plaintiffs, chosen to stand in for groups among the 600 women: Cook, Glueck, Eileen Shanahan and me for the news department; Louise Carini for clerical; Andrea Skinner, also from the news department, for all the women of color; and youthful Nancy Davis for the biggest bloc of the worst oppressed, the classified sales force.

Suing your employers is like suing for divorce and continuing to use the same bathroom. You know their visible stupidities. And we may be Joans of Arc, but we are not saints.

At a Christmas party during the suit, a man who remains a senior member of management lurched toward me in a doorway, pulled his index finger away from his glass and jabbed it at me. "You know why so-and-so isn't promoted?" he said. "She drinks." I said, "Tell you a secret: So do you." He does not remember that this happened.

After a company dinner for visiting U.N. delegates in the same period, a production bowwow with contempt for women was assigned to give me a tour of a big *Times* plant on the West Side at loading time. I was pleased with the off-street loading ramps because the tractor-trailers could no longer congest Times Square. "Great," I said, "those big boxes are off the street." "Bet you can't drive one the way men do," he said, adding a few other gibes about my ability to do a "man's job." I'll skip the rest and report that I drove a big hitch one cautious circuit inside the plant with dozens of supervisors and drivers as witnesses. We should both have been suspended for taking that kind of risk; he was later fired, probably for some other example of bad judgment.

Knowing that employees are prepared to testify to office practices and events such as the job slot held for an editor's bookmaker, paternity suits, tantrums, panic on deadline, ass-grabbing, locker-room drinking, multiple spouses in institutions and larceny, the managements go for the throat: They want to do everything they can to attack the abilities and the credibility of the witnesses who are their employees—us.

The anger of men who see breaches in the moat around their power zone is hard to contain. The vision of this sewer opening up in court is probably what kept any of the media cases from going to trial.

We underwent depositions by pit-bull lawyers, and our lawyers prepared us, as witnesses, for the sort of personal attacks they expected. Such experiences, piled upon careers of being underpaid, undervalued and refused promotions, tend to send leaders away. Rabb, when interviewed on television in the heat of the '70s, said conventional wisdom was that five years after a lawsuit, almost none of its leaders would still be in the same shops.

This was not our situation at the *Times*. Nancy Davis, the youngest and most mobile of us, left the *Times* in 1976, before settlement, seeking a better job after rejection for nine openings she had sought in *Times* ad sales. Eileen Shanahan, the most noted of us, in 1977 took a job as press spokeswoman in the Department of Health, Education and Welfare. (They are both still working.)

Then there were five.

Louise Carini continued as a benefits clerk until she retired at 65, in 1986, after 35 years at the *Times*. Grace Glueck, she of the unique talent, was promoted to art critic in 1982 and got a raise. But it was her last nonunion raise despite yearly requests for the nine years she remained. She attributes this to ageism rather than sexism or her role in the suit. She took the buyout at 65. Joan Cook, whose forte was as an assignment editor, was the most punished; after the paper stopped basing people in northern Jersey, where she had been assigned, she was shifted to day rewrite (meaning obituaries), a job without prestige, and continued to work for contract raises until she took the 1991 buyout at 69 years of age. Until Andrea Skinner took the 1991 buyout when she was 71, she continued to organize the children's fashion section from her misclassified slot as a news clerk, an injustice the management never cared to resolve. She got one raise in the period other than the yearly union raise.

It is said that Cook and I may have really undone our careers by leaping from the frying pan directly into an insurgent challenge for leadership of our union, the Newspaper Guild of New York, campaigning on the icy pavement outside the *Times* in December 1978 and winning easily. One flaw in this assumption is what happened to Howard Bishow and Joe Eisenberg, who had much earlier held two of the same union jobs. They were whisked off into management in triumph; Bishow's last *Times* post was as director of industrial relations, and Eisenberg was a heavy negotiator in the same department. Their golden handshakes were surely richer than Joan's.

But there's another flaw. The union establishment was as unenthusiastic about us as the management. The notion that we blighted our careers by union activism is merely a way of avoiding confronting our real problem: We are both politically on the left, reform-minded radicals who enraged the union leadership just as we enraged the *Times* management. In 1979, we were in the thick of an ultimately successful struggle to keep the Guild from again becoming involved in Latin American adventures using government—read "intelligence"—money. The paid union establishment, with help from the U.S. Department of Labor, rid itself of our leadership thereafter.

To get back to the arithmetic: two of seven left before settlement; four of the five others retired when they wanted, without citing the suit. I am the last still there, having received only union raises, plus a mandated raise when the management transferred me from the national desk to a different job classification in travel news.

The crucial reason we do not fit Rabb's rule of thumb is the Guild contract. I am often asked about fears of getting fired, and I reply I cannot imagine what our lives would have been without the contract, particularly its potential to summon an arbitration if the management had retaliated by complaining about our work. It would have embarrassed the *Times* publicly if an arbitrator heard that an overscale employee with a good record, prizes and recommendations over 20 years blew a whistle and suddenly became a stumblebum.

What do you do where there is no union? the potential plaintiffs cry. The risk is great, unless you marshal a group so large you cannot possibly all be picked off. The management has all the marbles.

What's it like staying on? "We became a source of information and embarrassment to our fellow workers," Cook says. "They treated us much as they always had, asking 'What do they want?' and yet they did not like to stand too close to us because some of it might rub off."

Cook, like me, considers the lawsuit and union leadership as a single flow of events, making it hard to know which aspect created the *cordon sanitaire* around us. Cook recalls the Hot New Young Talent who sat three rows away. Cook got a call from a friend on another floor saying she had a question from the H.N.Y.T. "Why can't she ask me herself?" Cook asked crossly. But then she provided the information, which was presumably relayed to the desk three rows away.

I sometimes told friends who were moving to the *Times* from other papers that they might not want to be seen talking to me, a position I think many union leaders adopt until a recruit's trial period is safely over. But in the time I was on the national desk, I was often asked to guide and supervise copy editors on tryout, so they got an earful about what to ask for and the going rates above the minimum.

Glueck says that her fellow workers had a "so what?" or grudging reaction after the suit. "I was proud of us," she says. "We achieved a victory and shook them up a bit. So I was hurt by the reaction of my colleagues. Basically they were shits."

In the settlement, we won an affirmative action plan for promotion and hiring that was supervised by the court for four years, and a cash settlement of $350,000, of which $233,500 went to the women—an average of $454 each, more than the *Reader's Digest* or NBC women got. It was distributed by seniority: from $100 for the newest employees up to $1,000 for those of us with more than 20 years. Glueck believes that the disdainful attitude of her colleagues derived from their belief that money was the objective, and the yield was poor.

The terms of the settlement were not widely known, but that was no accident. The *Times* came in with money offers in the last days of a strike that still had the *Times* and the *Daily News* shut down; there was coverage of the case as it ended, but a shadow of what it might have been. A researcher called me years later to ask what all the shouting was about, because he could not find the story in the *Times Index*. (For primary documents in the case, see *Media Report to Women* for the period 1974–78, available in libraries and from the former editor, Dr. Donna Allen, Women's Institute for Freedom of the Press, 3306 Ross Place, N.W., Washington, D.C. 20008, who, like the scribes of the Dark Ages, published a faithful record.)

Glueck, after appraising her colleagues' reactions, said: "The management people I worked for had a somewhat better attitude, that the suit was a good go. Of course, it did not affect them much. The young people? I began to resent that they had no sense of what had been done. Every 10 years, the same thing has to be done over again."

Cook demurs on the young. "Some of them, but not all" are ignorant of history. "And it is those few who will become leaders," she says.

"And the climate has changed. There is no longer one big newsroom—people are scattered all over and it is hard to get together, particularly to compare salaries. Young reporters tell you they'd love to come to the meeting but they are going to Italy to write a book that week. Their energies go into their careers. When you find leaders, they are over 40, when sex and children don't take all of their spare time.

"Organizing takes a lot of time," Cook concludes.

It is true that the motors of *Boylan v. Times* were over 40 when we realized that our careers were stalled: Joan and I were no longer wrestling with toilet training and reading readiness. Joan and Gerry Cook's children, and Jim Boylan's and mine, were increasingly autonomous, and while Gerry and Jim heard us come home late, both were staunchly behind our goals because of their finely tuned sense of justice. Gerry Cook was a decorated veteran of the Lincoln Battalion in Spain, as well as a veteran of World War II. He died in 1979. Jim Boylan was the one who looked at the first draft of the 1972 letter to the Sulzbergers and said: "Why are you asking for so little?"

Ten years after the settlement, in 1988, we held a party for ourselves, to enjoy the pat on the back that we all felt had not been forthcoming from our co-workers. We planned it and organized it and invited the speakers. Women holding jobs as photographers, art directors, sports reporters, mapmakers, assistant news editors, columnists— jobs never held by women before the suit—turned out. The mapmaker Emily Weiner, the coordinator of the women's caucus, convened it and then we stood back and basked. I cried when Anna Quindlen and E. R. Shipp and other brilliant young women looked at the record, perceived how the door was opened and pronounced our work historic.

But four years later we got in oversupply what we craved when Nan Robertson's *The Girls in the Balcony: Women, Men and the New York Times* was published by Random House. Letters, calls, embraces, encounters in halls, requests for speeches and autographs and citations at reunions. It is not a formula easily copied: You have to have a Pulitzer Prize winner like Robertson with a big talent, an editor who believes in her and a powerful publisher that is not afraid the *Times Book Review* will get even. But if you want the experience of stepping up from being a frog to being a prince, this is the way.

If they really do make a movie, story and characters will be mythological, but imagine what the grandchildren will think!

Toward the end of her book, Robertson cites a 1990 interview with Arthur Ochs Sulzberger Jr., who became publisher of the *Times* two years later. Flipping sheets of statistics, he said that women's salaries were catching up, and that the newest employees were benefiting most.

"In 1987," Robertson wrote, "the average salary of men in the news division hired within the previous five years was $13,000 higher than the average salary of women hired in the same period; in 1990 there was no gap between the average starting salary of men and that of women in the division."

In November 1992, the women's caucus of the *Times* received from the Newspaper Guild a salary tape that had been provided by the newspaper as required in advance of contract bargaining. The caucus got a computer professional to squeeze some comparisons out of the tape. The expert rounded off all the salaries to the nearest $1 to be sure no one could recognize anyone else, and started in the news department, where pay scales traditionally run above the Guild minimums, and where the sex differentials thus show up.

The worst gap showed at the top of the *Times* scale in pay Group O—the level above reporter-editor Group 10—encompassing national correspondents, desk heads, assistant desk heads, critics, columnists and others. The figures for employees with one to four years' experience—the same group Sulzberger was dealing with in 1990—showed the average male weekly salary at $1,466 and the average female salary at $1,319. That is, the women starting out in these good jobs were earning 11 percent less than the men. My calculator puts the annual gap between these numbers at $7,644. The Guild salary minimum in this category after six months on the job was $1,307 at the time, meaning the men were averaging $8,268 a year above the minimum and the women $624.

In the four-year period that the court enforced the terms of the affirmative action program, we discovered, the widening of the male-female salary gap slowed. When that period ended, though, the gap resumed its leaps and bounds. What the new caucus figures show is that women get shortchanged on arrival, in the initial offer from the *Times*. The caucus has little power to reach these women to tell them to hold out for more in the beginning. There is no way to catch up later.

Cook, Glueck and I, aside from sharing profound affection for each other and belly laughs that surprise cabbies, also share the belief that our work together and the process of the suit, rather than its outcome, formed us.

Glueck says it was the most important action of her professional life. "Along with Gerry," Cook says, "it was my source of a sense of history and a sense of principle. It gave me a sense of self."

I started out afraid, but with friends like that, who can remain timid? *Boylan v. Times* made me a tiger.

Betsy Wade, one of seven named plaintiffs in the 1973 landmark sex discrimination suit against the New York Times, *writes the* Times' *"The Practical Traveler" column. This chapter originally appeared in the winter/spring 1993* Media Studies Journal, *"The Media and Women Without Apology."*

7

Requiem for the Boys on the Bus

Maureen Dowd

Howie Kurtz is a nutcake. I mean, listen to what Kurtz, the media reporter for the *Washington Post,* had to say about how women have ruined all the fun of political reporting, compared to the raffish old days celebrated by Timothy Crouse 21 years ago in *The Boys on the Bus.*

"The '92 Zeitgeist has clearly shifted," Kurtz wrote last fall, "because the increasing prominence of women reporters has all but ended the locker-room high jinks chronicled in Crouse's book."

That is such a crock. It's enough to make a gal reach for the comfort of a Jack Daniel's and a pack of Viceroys.

Kurtz has it all backwards. It's guys who are ruining political journalism. Trust me.

Before the new breed of New Age stiffs came on the campaign bus in the last few years, things were different. I could go out and have a couple of pops at an after-hours joint with my pal Alessandra Stanley of the *New York Times.* I could play blackjack on the campaign plane with Ann McDaniel of *Newsweek.* I could stop by an OTB parlor with Ann Devroy of the *Washington Post* and we could pick a good horse in the eighth.

Now, the road is filled with a bunch of 30–something, touchy-feely guys, tying up all the cellular phone circuits trying to call home to talk baby talk to their wives and kids. "Hi, pumpkin!" coos Tom Friedman, the straight-arrow White House reporter for the *New York Times*. (He addresses his wife and both daughters as "pumpkin," if you can believe it.)

The worst was last Halloween, the weekend before the presidential election. We had been on a train going nowhere with George Bush all day in Wisconsin, meandering around the state seeing cows and a few voters. When we finally got on the bus to our hotel, around 9 p.m., Michael Kranish of the *Boston Globe* and Michael Wines of the *New York Times* kept trying to call home on their cell phones. Then they started getting all misty about how they wished they could have been back in D.C. with their kids for Halloween. They were jealous of John Harwood of the *Wall Street Journal*, who had already bailed out, telling his editors he had to be home on Halloween.

Wines got really upset when he found out his little boy, who was dressing up as an airplane, had broken one of his wings and Daddy wasn't there to fix it. Then Kranish lost it when his 5–year-old daughter pressed him on the phone about why he couldn't come home that night.

In the dumps, Kranish resorted to taking a sip of a beer. "Whew," he said. "This is really going to my head. We don't drink much at home anymore. After I go running, I might have a lite beer or a nonalcoholic beer."

SHEEEESH! Thanks for sharing, Mike.

I mean, whatever happened to the venerable old code that venerable old political reporters once lived by—"Wheels up, rings off!" And "Never order more than two dry martinis before dinner unless you can see the table from where you're standing."

Not only that. These guys look like such trolls, in their uniform of navy blazers, khaki trousers and rep ties. TIES! They're well coiffed and they have waistlines—they might as well be television reporters! They show not the slightest shame about droning on about such sissy topics as infant formula, Nautilus machines, jogging trails and lipoprotein levels.

When there were more of us tough babes around, we used to have fun. We composed satirical songs, parodied the candidate's stump speech, took the pols out to the nearest Holiday Inn cocktail lounge to drink until 2 a.m.

The new guys? They don't care about songs or steak dinners. They're too busy quizzing each other along these lines: "Do you have an internal fax modem?" "If you don't have 9600 baud, why bother?" "With battery life such a huge problem, if you don't have nickel hydride, why get on the plane?" "Don't you find a Gateway 2000 handbook a godsend on long flights?"

The blue-blazer crowd could care less about the inside baseball of politics or about handicapping the horse race anymore. They can't touch my colleague, Robin Toner, when it comes to dissecting an electoral map. These Iron John dweebs all want to write their damn fingers off about personality stuff, color stuff.

I mean, you pick up the *New York Times* during the campaign and there's Andrew Rosenthal writing about fashion, for chrissake! Rosenthal wrote a whole story about George Bush's windbreaker: "Supplied by the Air Force, this ultimate symbol of Washington status is available to only the most select clientele: Presidents. It is generally worn on Air Force One, the President's aircraft, where the chief executive slips it over his dress shirt and telegenic ties for that relaxed-but-still-in-command look."

Like other high-cholesterol items, meat-and-potatoes leads are a thing of the past. Look at how Michael Kelly of the *New York Times* started his story on the Richmond presidential debate, the one featuring a talk show format where Bush, Clinton and Perot took questions from the studio audience: "It turns out there is a reason Phil Donahue likes to talk to cannibalistic transsexuals in love with their mothers. . . . Historic, the debate was. Also responsible, civic-minded, worthwhile and informative. Also as dull as C-SPAN at midnight."

And here's Jack Farrell, the F. Scott of the *Boston Globe*, describing candidate Bill Clinton as "a man who goes jogging in a *Rolling Stone* sweatshirt and then scarfs down slices of Pizza Hut pizza—the Meat Lover's special, no less—with the tech crews and cameramen in the galley of his airplane. From his acknowledgment of a troubled marriage to his junk-food appetite, to the blowzy speeches he gave at the 1988 and 1992 Democratic conventions, Clinton seems to speak of a generation's self-indulgence."

Speaking of self-indulgence, WHAT ABOUT THE ISSUES, Jack?

I know. I sound like a curmudgeon. But these guys get to me. They're the ones who don't want to have fun, who just want to stay in their rooms and write cutesy features on their high-tech computers.

Come on, Howie, you bum, you're full of bull, blaming the broads for ending "locker-room high jinks." It's you guys, the Bores on the Bus.

Cripes! I give up. I'm going to the racetrack.

Maureen Dowd is a White House political correspondent and columnist for the New York Times. *This chapter originally appeared in the winter/spring 1993* Media Studies Journal, *"The Media and Women Without Apology."*

8

The Best Seat in the House?

Lawrence K. Grossman

Premiere in Flatbush

The place to sit on an opening night at the Metropolitan Opera is a Parterre Box just above the main floor, or the Grand Tier one level higher still, or Bickford's Cafeteria, across the street on Seventh Avenue. At Bickford's 50 to 80 chauffeurs cluster over English muffins and coffee cups until their employers decamp from the Grand Tier and the Parterre Boxes. The chauffeurs know their opera and their composers. They detest Richard Wagner. 'Those Germans go on all night.' They love Puccini. 'He always lets out by 10:30.' And they never see either. But the Sunday afternoon of March 3 will make history, for this time, the chauffeurs, like the chic and millions of other Americans, will see the grandest of curtain raisers: the world premiere of an opera. . . . And this time every music lover, every drama lover—not to mention every muffin-cloyed, coffee-sated chauffeur—can have the best seat in the house.

Twenty-seven years ago, before the Met moved to Lincoln Center, those words appeared in a full-page advertisement in the *New Yorker* bought by NBC to celebrate the world premiere of a modern opera— Gian Carlo Menotti's *The Labyrinth*. It was the 57th NBC opera production to be televised over a span of 12 seasons. *The Labyrinth*, produced in the network's Flatbush studios, was not an especially memorable work, and as far as I know has not been seen since. But that NBC televised any grand opera at all, let alone 57 operas over 12 seasons, is worth noting today.

The author of that advertisement, incidentally, was a young *New York Herald Tribune* reporter named Tom Wolfe, who had just come to the city to make his reputation. I was in charge of NBC's advertising at the time and commissioned Tom to write the copy, which expressed the vision many of us working in television then shared: to give "every music lover, every drama lover" and everyone else who otherwise never would have had the opportunity "the best seat in the house" for culturally enriching fare—from Euripides to Eugene O'Neill, from Bach to Balanchine. We had high hopes for television in those early days.

There has always been a certain dissonance between the mass appeal of commercial television and the elite taste of high culture. In his 1974 book *Popular Culture and High Culture*, the sociologist Herbert Gans wrote, "In America, as in all Western societies, the longest and perhaps most important cultural struggle has pitted the educated practitioners of high culture against most of the rest of society, rich and poor, which prefers the mass or popular culture provided by the mass media and the consumer goods industry." Or, as classical music impresario Sol Hurok put it, "If people do not want to come, nothing can stop them."

Still, the early broadcasters felt they had both a responsibility and a unique opportunity to use the new electronic media to elevate as well as to entertain the masses. The question was not whether commercial broadcasters should carry the fine arts, but what the ratio of high culture to popular entertainment should be. Today that question is asked no longer. The fine arts have all but disappeared from commercial television, and the ideal of a "best seat in the house" for all is dead.

There are, to be sure, one or two reminders: the occasional reports on classical music and modern jazz given by Eugenia Zuckerman and

Billy Taylor on Charles Kuralt's civilized "Sunday Morning" program on CBS; Bill Cosby's tribute to the late Alvin Ailey on NBC (which was actually as much a tribute to Cosby's tremendous contractual clout with NBC as it was to Ailey's choreography); and on cable, the program schedules of BRAVO and the A&E channel, both of which contain far more entertainment than fine arts, and mostly inexpensive imports at that.

Despite commercial television's glitter and showmanship, the industry today is all business and the bottom line. Its managers and new owners care little about their audience's cultural improvement. General Electric, which acquired NBC in 1986 along with RCA, regards broadcasting as "just another product line"—a view that was reinforced when GE sold NBC Radio to Westwood One along with the right to put the NBC News label on Westwood's own news programming, just as GE sold the right to put the GE and RCA labels on television and radio sets manufactured by other companies.

The single-minded mission of commercial TV today is to produce audiences for sale to advertisers. What gets on the air is whatever will attract viewers, which means entertainment that provides instant gratification, relaxation, excitement and escape. The fine arts, by contrast, tend to require thought, discipline, concentration, seriousness of purpose and educated attention. These elitist demands commercial television is in no position to satisfy. Moreover, high culture's aesthetic values bear almost no relationship to television's marketplace criteria of cost-per-thousand, Nielsen ratings and youthful demographics, and are usually incompatible with television's pattern of frequent commercial interruption.

That commercial broadcasting would be driven solely by marketplace demands was not the original vision of the industry's founders. In the early 1920s General David Sarnoff, the first president of RCA, saw radio as a "music box" on which the public "could enjoy concerts, lectures, music, recitals." Secretary of Commerce Herbert Hoover, who regulated the industry before the 1927 Radio Law was passed, said it was "inconceivable that we should allow so great a possibility for service . . . to be drowned in advertising chatter." Broadcasting was meant to combine business and public service, commerce and art. It promised to inform, educate and uplift as well as entertain the population; to be the great equalizing and elevating force in our democratic society.

From commercial radio's beginnings in the late 1920s, a Faustian bargain was struck between the government and broadcasters. The government granted broadcasters monopoly licenses to operate on the scarce and valuable public airwaves. In return broadcasters promised to program their stations "in the public interest, convenience and necessity," which meant scheduling concerts, drama, opera, news and public affairs as well as popular entertainment and sports, for the benefit of *all* the people. The Federal Radio Commission and its successor agency, the Federal Communications Commission, were to examine each licensee's record at renewal time to make sure that the public interest was being served.

The industry's formal commitment to integrate the arts into the mainstream was made in the early 1930s in response to a powerful lobbying effort by educational, religious and other nonprofit organizations, which even then were concerned about the squeezing out of noncommercial educational stations by commercial ones. Although the FRC had concluded that "educational" programming could safely be left in the hands of commercial broadcasters whose capacity and willingness to provide for it would "far exceed the demand," a congressional amendment to the 1934 Communications Act nearly gave educational, religious, agricultural, labor and other nonprofit associations and cooperatives 25 percent of all radio frequencies for cultural and informational use. These nonprofit broadcasters would have solicited advertising sponsors just like commercial ones did.

The crucial amendment was defeated in Congress but the new FCC was asked to study the proposal as its first order of business. After taking extensive testimony from commercial broadcasters, who pledged that large percentages of their programming would be devoted to such uplifting purposes, the Commission reported back to Congress that there was no need for separate nonprofit facilities. "It would appear that the interests of the nonprofit organizations may be better served by the use of existing facilities, thus giving them access to costly and efficient equipment and to established audiences," the agency said.

It was in this climate that NBC created, in 1937, its own world-class symphony orchestra for the sole purpose of enticing the celebrated Italian conductor Arturo Toscanini to come to the United States and broadcast concerts to the entire nation. The network hired the prominent composer and musical scholar Dr. Walter Damrosch to lecture and perform on radio. Impresario Samuel Chotzinoff was brought aboard to produce Toscanini and the NBC operas. After World War II, when the FM spectrum finally opened up, it was expected that special-interest audiences would be served even more effectively. Hundreds of additional radio stations with high-fidelity sound would allow concerts, drama and fine arts programming to proliferate. The nation's symphony orchestras, opera companies and arts organizations readied themselves for the expected bonanza of bigger audiences, new performing opportunities and increased revenues from radio.

The early days of television featured grand opera, the weekly arts show "Omnibus" and dramatic series such as "Studio One," "Playhouse 90," "Philco Playhouse," "Kraft Television," "Armstrong Circle Theater," "The Alcoa Hour" "and "The U.S. Steel Hour," all of which vied to produce distinguished original material and nurtured a generation of outstanding American playwrights and directors, including Paddy Chayefsky, Reginald Rose, Rod Serling, Gore Vidal, Robert Alan Arthur, J.P. Miller, William Gibson, John Frankenheimer, Franklin Schaffner and Sidney Lumet. These years are now known as the "Golden Age of Television," and while there is undoubtedly excessive nostalgia in this description, an exceptional number of programs of high artistic and cultural merit appeared side-by-side with Milton Berle, "Father Knows Best," "Gunsmoke" and "Strike It Rich."

But that promising start came to naught in the late 1950s. And in the '70s and '80s, when a new era of television station abundance on UHF and cable channels renewed the hope that cultural programs would flourish, the reverse occurred. Perversely, the proliferation of broadcasting channels provided a far less friendly environment for the fine arts than ever existed in the old days of station scarcity and network dominance. Commercial radio and television have become a fine arts desert. On commercial radio there is little musical diversity, hardly any original concert performances, no drama, no poetry, no educational programming and no sustained discussion of the arts. And commercial television is traveling down the same road, propelled by the same forces: channel abundance and deregulation.

How did it happen that the arts, which mankind values as essential to a civilized society, have lost their place in the nation's most pervasive, influential and important media of communications? In an age driven relentlessly by market forces, the classic explanation was supplied by the critic Dwight Macdonald: "There seems to be a Gresham's Law in cultural as well as currency circulation: Bad stuff drives out the good, and the worst drives out the bad. For the bad is more easily enjoyed than the good—in fact, it is this facility of access which at once sells it on a wide market and also prevents it from achieving quality."

But there is more to it than Gresham's Law applied to culture. The very abundance of radio and television channels has intensified the competition for viewers and listeners in a way that cuts into the size of the audience that any one channel can attract and reduces the commercial broadcaster's willingness and ability to pay for costly, noncompetitive cultural programming. True, television today offers more choices now that dozens of channels instead of only three or four are available in each market. But that diversity is limited to what advertisers and cable operators are willing to pay for, namely blockbuster entertainment, sports and news. The brief history of cable TV is littered with failed performing arts channels. CBS Cable, ARTS and the Entertainment Channel, all originated by old-line network broadcasters hoping to improve television and make money in cable, died quick and expensive deaths—or were merged into less ambitious services.

This should come as no surprise. The fine arts have required private or public subsidy to flourish since at least the Renaissance. Individual artists like Michelangelo, Mozart, Haydn, Wagner and Verdi, and collective organizations like symphony orchestras, dance, opera and drama companies have always had to depend on princes, prelates and patrons in order to survive. That is why the expectation that commercial broadcasters would, in effect, subsidize the placement of the arts and public affairs programming on their schedules became embedded in the FCC's public interest standard. The economic and social justification for imposing that standard was the scarcity of radio and television station licenses to operate on the public airwaves.

With the explosion in the number of stations, the old reliance on the federal public interest standard was gradually replaced by the conviction that market forces would take care of all needs. Someone would surely make room for high culture, went the new line. Old-line broadcasters argued that it was unfair and unnecessary for the government to require them to provide costly cultural programming while their cable and videocassette competition got a free ride. So the principle of a free market deposed the public-service standard, and deregulation became the policy of the day. And commercial broadcasters retain their valuable licenses to the public airwaves, which have grown even more valuable now that they are no longer encumbered by FCC public-service requirements or FCC limits on when and how they can be bought and sold.

The deregulation of broadcasting began under Jimmy Carter and was carried forward, with great ideological enthusiasm and for somewhat different reasons, under Ronald Reagan. The Carter FCC believed that deregulation would promote diversity of ownership, especially among minorities and independent broadcasters, thus producing more programming diversity and reducing the power of the three national networks. The Reagan FCC believed that the federal government should get out of the business of regulating and setting standards for private industry in the conviction that free market forces would fill our needs better than government bureaucrats.

Now we depend entirely on *public* broadcasting to fill the cultural void. In recent years, public radio and television have been the nation's one consistent and reliable source for performing-arts programming. This is a far cry from the FCC's original (if unrealistic) goal of integrating art and commerce within mainstream commercial broadcasting. Ours is the only country whose public broadcasting system arrived as an afterthought, years after commercial radio and television had already gained the upper hand. By contrast, other nations' broadcasting systems began as government-operated and -controlled monopolies, with privatization a relatively recent phenomenon.

The worldwide preference for government-run radio and television has reflected government's determination to control the immense power of broadcasting in its own interest more than any impulse to use radio and television to elevate public taste or promote the national arts and culture. But the latter impulse unquestionably has helped determine most countries' broadcasting priorities, especially those nations with a long history of public subsidy of the arts. As part of its regular programming, for example, the BBC has funded the Scottish, Welsh and BBC symphony orchestras and many playwrights, performing artists, musicians and poets, including such well-known figures as Harold Pinter, Tom Stoppard and Alan Ayckbourn.

The United States, on the other hand, has a historic suspicion of government involvement in the media and not much of a tradition of government support of the performing arts. Noncommercial public broadcasting was not even launched here until 1952, and its initial mandate was strictly educational. Consistent with the U.S. tradition of local control and local financing of public education, educational broadcasting began at local stations with no interconnected national network and no federal money. No significant role was foreseen for culture or the performing arts.

Ironically, much of the leadership of educational broadcasting during those first years came from the nation's poorest states, which saw in television technology a dramatic opportunity to leapfrog over their backward educational systems and make major improvements at modest cost. The most sophisticated and the best-equipped educational television systems were built first in states like South Carolina, Mississippi, Maine and New Hampshire, and the people in charge were educators rather than broadcasters.

It was not until 1967, with the landmark *Report of the Carnegie Commission on Educational Television*, that a broad-based concept of public television was introduced in this country. The Commission, launched with the blessing of President Lyndon Johnson, recommended that the United States have "a civilized voice" on television, one that would provide "a fuller awareness of the wonder and the variety of the arts." For the first time some funding came from the federal government: Johnson proposed a modest $4.5 million. More federal funds began to flow slowly in the early 1970s, but long-term support was not actually made available until 1976, when President Gerald Ford signed a $78.5 million multiyear funding bill. The arts at last were given a home of their own, albeit separate and poorly financed, on American radio and television.

For the past 15 years public television has offered a wide variety of cultural programming: arts documentaries, original drama on the "American Playhouse" series and opera, concerts and dance on "Great Performances" and "Live From Lincoln Center." Still, there are huge gaps. The vast body of 20th-century American dramas by Eugene O'Neill, Tennessee Williams, Arthur Miller, William Inge and others, for example, has never been produced on public television. And many of the cultural and arts programs on PBS are imports, predominantly British. (One wonders where American public television would be if the British didn't speak English.) Nor has public television developed a reputation for artistic boldness. Its programming decisions tend to be cautious and conventional (and were that way when I ran PBS).

American public television's most distinctive contribution to the arts, in my mind, has been its dance programming, particularly the exceptional "Dance in America" series. Now in its 14th season, the series has helped spur an American dance renaissance. "Dance in America" produces an average of four new programs a year and has amassed an extraordinarily distinguished body of work.

Even though "Dance in America" is one of public television's great success stories, its continuing funding problems illustrate some of the weaknesses of the PBS system. "Dance in America" began in 1976 with seed money from the National Endowment for the Arts, but millions of dollars in matching grants had to be raised before it could continue beyond its first season. After a long search, the Corporation for Public Broadcasting, the recipient of the federal funds, together with the oil company Exxon, agreed to put up the necessary underwriting. But in the early 1980s, CPB tried to withdraw its funding on the grounds that financing should be sought from other sources now that "Dance in America" had become well established. No other major underwriters could be found to share credit with Exxon and step into CPB's place, so CPB reluctantly decided to renew its grants on a somewhat reduced scale. Then Exxon, after more than a decade of support, ended its commitment, citing its own financial troubles. Another long and frustrating scramble for money resulted in additional funding from local public television stations and from Martin Marietta, a defense contractor. But this now provides only one-third to one-half of "Dance in America's" annual budget. While constantly looking over their shoulders at their existing commitments, the producers have continually had to shake the tambourine with foundations and develop overseas co-production deals. A growing corps of foreign broadcasters and distributors has stepped in to fill the gap, but at times the cost has been the surrender of overseas rights and some loss of creative control. Some foreign funding has taken the form of in-kind production deals, which means that episodes of "Dance in America" have had to be produced in Europe using foreign talent.

While the United States has lagged far behind Britain and other nations in government subsidies to the arts and public broadcasting, our cultural gap is now beginning to narrow. Federal support for the National Endowment for the Arts and public broadcasting has consistently grown even during the austere Reagan years when many other domestic programs were severely gutted or eliminated altogether. The annual federal appropriation for public broadcasting, including satellite funding, is almost $300 million; for the NEA it is more than $170 million. These increases are testimony to the political clout of our performing arts institutions. They also reflect public recognition of the need to make up for the cultural deficit that commercial broadcasting has left in the wake of deregulation.

Meanwhile, in Britain and other nations the trend has been to de-emphasize government-supported broadcasting in favor of privatization. Under Margaret Thatcher, the BBC has had to pare down its substantial orchestra support and much of its cultural patronage and may even face the prospect of becoming self-supporting some day. In this regard the United States and Britain are moving in opposite directions.

Still, in this country there is a strong current of opposition to any government financing, which centers on three arguments:

1. *In the multichannel environment, government subsidies are no longer needed. The marketplace is supposed to satisfy whatever cultural aspirations society may have.*

On the contrary, the experience of the past decade, not to mention the past several centuries, demonstrates that the fine arts are unable to pay their own way, no matter what the economic system or the state of technology. If the marketplace ever does enable the fine arts to flourish within the landscape of television, the question of public subsidy can be revisited. But past performance does not offer any hope for that happening.

2. *Public financing of the arts inevitably brings with it undue government interference and an unacceptable threat to artistic freedom.*

The concern about government interference is well taken and raises an important issue. The recent imbroglio between North Carolina Sen. Jesse Helms and the National Endowment for the Arts over its support of the Robert Mapplethorpe exhibit demonstrates just how difficult it is for a government agency to fund unorthodox ideas and for the Congress to keep from meddling in what it finances by requiring accountability (not an unreasonable requirement, by the way).

In fact, however, over the years the record of insulation from government intrusion into artistic or programming content has been surprisingly good, and there have been remarkably few instances of federal officials restricting artistic freedom or stomping on unconventional ideas. One reason is that both the NEA and public broadcasting have been structured in complicated ways to insulate themselves from political interference. Both use elaborate panel grant mechanisms and have multilayered, decentralized decision-making processes.

These structures and processes are so complex, and often so bureaucratic, that it is a miracle they work at all. The Corporation for Public Broadcasting, the recipient of the federal appropriation for public broadcasting, is prohibited by law from producing its own programs and operating its own network. The public broadcasting networks, PBS and National Public Radio, are kept independent from CPB because they are owned and controlled by the individual public stations throughout the country. And to give PBS programming even more insulation from politicians in Washington, the network is prohibited by its corporate charter from producing the programs it distributes.

The idea is that there should be no single place that any government official can go to influence what programs get on public broadcasting. However, even the most elaborately complex structure can occasionally be penetrated—as in the early 1970s when Nixon White House aides tried to kill all of PBS's public affairs programming, and in 1980 when the Carter State Department attempted to dissuade PBS from televising a docudrama that offended the Saudi government. Neither effort succeeded.

There has also been some reluctance by public broadcasting itself to fund controversial and unorthodox programs, perhaps out of concern about how Congress might react. However, the main problem so far has not been too much federal meddling but too little federal funding.

3. *In this time of budget deficits and intense pressure to reduce public spending, government funds should be used only to serve our most pressing human needs. Compared to the growing problems of drugs, crime, the homeless, inner-city poverty, public education and the environment, federal support for the arts is a luxury we can no longer afford. And why should the poor pay taxes to subsidize the arts that mostly benefit the rich?*

This argument, which has a certain populist appeal, presupposes a rather pinched view of the public agenda. As the historian Arthur Schlesinger Jr. said in the first annual Nancy Hanks Lecture on Arts and Public Policy in 1988: "Is it not the real elitism to suggest that low-income people have no interest in the arts and can derive no benefit from public support of the higher arts? Surely the poor as well as the better off have appetites to be awakened . . . lives to be illuminated. . . . Surely, the government has as strong an obligation to preserve the cultural environment against dissipation and destruction as it has to preserve the national environment against pollution and decay."

History will measure our nation's achievements not by our wealth or the superiority of our free-market forces, but by our cultural legacy and the character of our civilization. Ironically, it was in the depths of the Great Depression when resources were far scarcer than they are today that the federal government first made the arts and the nation's artists a priority for national public support. Today the New Deal's arts projects rank among its most memorable achievements.

During the 1990s and beyond, in the absence of a major global conflict or a new Cold War, improvement of the quality of American life inevitably will become the nation's most important public priority. Increasing support for the creative and performing arts, and for the publicly funded electronic media that make them accessible to all the people, is inevitable. Bickford's Cafeteria, the *New York Herald Tribune* and NBC Opera are long gone. But in the decade ahead, despite the marketplace mentality and the increase in channel capacity, public television and radio are destined to play an increasingly important role in making the arts a significant part of our national life. For that is where "every music lover, every drama lover—not to mention every muffin-cloyed, coffee-sated chauffeur" will have to find the "best seat in the house."

Lawrence K. Grossman is the former president of PBS and NBC News and is currently president of the PBS Horizons Cable Network. He is the author of The Electronic Republic. *This chapter originally appeared in the winter 1990* Media Studies Journal, *"Arts & Media."*

9

From Pollock to Mapplethorpe—
The Media and the Artworld

Arthur C. Danto

Somewhere, yellowing if it can yellow further, brittle no doubt as old wallpaper, I have the clipped page from *Life* magazine from which, into my consciousness as into that of millions of others, Jackson Pollock's sullen and explosive presence became an urgent reality. The clipping is somewhere, if I care to root through dusty folders to find it, but the image remains, vivid in my memory, of the artist glowering out of the page through narrowed eyes, cigarette hanging from lips set in a slanted snarl, arms crossed protectively across chest, legs crossed as well, standing in paint-splashed work clothes with, behind him, the whorled cursive of looped paint across a severely horizontal canvas that seemed nearly endless, as it was cropped at both edges by the sheet it was printed on. Pollock is poised arrogantly before a work no less arrogant than himself in scale and pictorial ambition, as if projecting an affirmative answer to the rhetorical question splashed beneath the name. From that moment forward he became part of the cultural currency in the little enclave I inhabited in Detroit as an undergraduate on the GI Bill at Wayne State University—a name now mentioned as frequently as Picasso's, or Freud's or Joyce's.

The question was: "Is he the greatest living painter in the United States?" and Pollock's feet are planted on the same line as the print, between the words "greatest" and "living," and his figure rises up from the sentence like an interstitial exclamation point, punctuationally overriding the question mark at the end.

That question defined the shape of discussion for a long while in my world in Detroit, and it was surely through the to-and-fro of provincial controversy to which the question gave rise that the resolution formed itself in my will to move to New York City. There, I realized, art was something that was happening, and really at no other place in the world. At a stroke, *Life* had dissolved all the little centers where a person like myself lived happily enough within the horizons of local artworlds and melted it all into a single artistic culture with one luminous center. The artists who lived at that center—Willem de Kooning, Franz Kline, Robert Motherwell, Mark Rothko, Barnett Newman—whose internal experience of the life of art in New York cannot have differed greatly from my own internal sense of the life of art in Detroit, became abruptly enlarged into national creative deities, as disproportionate to the artists I locally admired as Apollo and Zeus would be to Sarpedon and Diomedes. Even the best painters in Detroit diminished into talented eccentrics, beached by the sweep of history.

I do not know when the expression "the Artworld" came into general usage. I appropriated it as the title for a paper published in *The Journal of Philosophy* in October 1964 (I had gone on to become a philosopher rather than a painter), in which I laid the groundwork for what came to be called The Institutional Theory of Art, which said, in essence, that to see something as art requires more than vision; it requires mastery of a certain discourse and knowledge of the history of art. In retrospect, it seems to me that the germ of my theory was already there, in the provocative engagement between reader, image and text on that extraordinary page in *Life*, though in truth the artworld itself, partly under the impact of that page, had itself changed drastically by 1964.

Pollock, of course, was dead. He was famous enough, in 1956, that I learned of the accident listening to the news over an obscure radio station in northern Vermont, near the Canadian border, where the announcer, who called himself "Cousin Harold, the Hired Hand," reported it along with the items of intelligence more immediately relevant to his rural auditors. But even more significantly, Abstract Expressionism, which the movement Pollock belonged to was known as by then, was itself dead, to be replaced by something no one could have imagined.

"The Artworld" was a philosophical response to an exhibition that had made an immense impact upon me, of simulacra of cardboard cartons, especially of Brillo boxes, that Andy Warhol had shown the previous spring at the Stable Gallery on East 74th Street in New York. There were hundreds of these "cartons" piled in an array that would be familiar to most Americans who had looked into the stockrooms of supermarkets but was radically unfamiliar in an art gallery. What fascinated me—what came to obsess me philosophically—was why these were taken as works of art while the objects in the stockrooms, which resembled them in any relevant respect, were simply what they were— containers for soap-pads. Sidney Tillim, the artist and critic, wrote in *Arts Magazine* of the Brillo boxes as "a gesture of aggressive passivity. . . . The visual emptiness of it all is the price [Warhol] seems willing to pay for an instant of sublime but compulsive negation." Nothing remotely like that language would have been appropriate in describing mere Brillo cartons, in which Americans mailed books or shipped dishes or bedded kittens down, when they were discarded by the A&P. And this was true even though the actual workaday Brillo carton was designed by James Harvey, a "second generation" Abstract Expressionist who took to commercial art. The question of the philosophical nature of art was being raised from within the artworld.

Whether and why something is art (when something that looks just like it is a mere pasteboard artifact) is, as a question, markedly more philosophical than the question of who the greatest living painter is. But the graphic genius of *Life*'s format could easily have been adapted to the situation of 1964 were *Life* still, in that year, the great transformative mass magazine it had been in 1949 when the article on Pollock changed so many lives. Imagine the photograph by Fred W. McDarrah of Warhol standing amidst stacks of Brillo boxes above the printed question "Is he the greatest living artist in the United States?" The contrast between the two physiognomies, with Warhol looking like a waif under his signature mop of blond hair and seeming to shrink into a makeshift fortress of piled boxes, serves as an index to transformations in styles of artistic presence, from hot to cool, from gunslinger to window dresser, from jazz to philosophical cerebration. And the artworks themselves mark the same transformation. But the provocation aimed at the common reader would have been much the same. To put a question about the shown artist and art in superlatives of a nearly Barnum dimension, when the work was so unlike anything the reader was prepared, in the case of Pollock, to regard as painting and, in that of Warhol, to regard as art, was surely intended to elicit a NO! in the reader's mind. At the same time it gave rise to the further question of why the question was being asked. And were the reader to have gone to the text, she or he would be further provoked to discover that there were authorities who believed the answer to be YES!

In the case of Pollock, the first line of the article was, "Recently a formidable highbrow New York critic hailed the brooding, puzzled-looking man above as a major artist of our time and as a fine candidate for 'The Greatest American Painter of the Twentieth Century.'" The unnamed critic of course was Clement Greenberg, who did that hailing in *The Partisan Review* or *The Nation*. My imagined *Life* page on Warhol might have cited a professor of philosophy in a highbrow New York college. I did not say in *The Journal of Philosophy* what I was to say 25 years later (having become Greenberg's successor as art critic for *The Nation*), that "Warhol is the nearest thing to a philosophical genius the history of art has so far produced." But if the article had appeared, it is not difficult to suppose the line would have sounded simply crazy in 1964—as crazy, perhaps, as Greenberg must have sounded to many of *Life*'s readers in 1949.

There is a fair amount of rhetoric in the *Life* essay on Jackson Pollock: Words like "highbrow," "formidable" and "New York" are not calculated to elicit reverence and awe in the lower-middle-class American soul. But the display of the work (the painting was Pollock's "Summertime": 9a, 1948, now one of the treasures of the Tate Gallery), together with a question that was, given the background assumptions of the reader, required to sound extravagant, had to have engaged the reader's mind and ought to have prodded the reader, after his or her explosive negation, to think what possible reason a formidable highbrow authority might have for so preposterous a view. (It might have been reassuring to have quoted Pollock's own uncertainty as to whether what he had achieved was really painting, as his wife, Lee Krasner, remembered him doing in her moving memoir.) Looking more closely will not greatly help either, and certainly not with the parallel question of 1964. Whatever may be the physical differences between a Warhol Brillo box and a carton for Brillo (the differences between plywood and corrugated cardboard, for example), a photograph of the one looks the same as a photograph of the other. And people I knew, even (or especially) artists, were pretty angered by the Stable exhibit. One painter I know, romantic and impulsive, scribbled an obscenity across a page of the guest book. Years later I said to him, "The difference between us is that you wrote 'Shit!' and I wrote *The Transfiguration of the Commonplace*"—the book that grew out of my essay "The Artworld."

"To see something as art requires something the eye cannot decry— an atmosphere of artistic theory, a knowledge of the history of art: an artworld," I had written in that essay. These words were the foundations for the Institutional Theory of Art, and they certainly have been the most widely quoted words I have ever written, before or since. What the reader of *Life* was missing was a knowledge of the kind of theory through which Pollock was enfranchised as a great painter, and the history against which his achievement had to be perceived as an astonishing breakthrough. What the reader in Detroit—and everywhere else outside a few square blocks in Manhattan and a few square miles in Long Island—lacked was the kind of knowledge those defined as part of the artworld possess. Needless to say, not everyone in the artworld would have agreed with Greenberg. John Canaday, the awful critic of the *New York Times*, loathed Abstract Expressionism and did what he could to kill it (its death was not due to him). And Hilton Kramer, his acidulous successor in that post, loathed Warhol to an even higher degree. Still, both of these critics were participants in a discourse that the mass media audience could not know of and to which it did not belong.

My thought, subsequently taken up and developed in the work of George Dickie, is that there is an informal tribunal of persons for whom art matters enough that questions of what art is and when art is great and what constitutes a breakthrough are matters of continuing discussion and argument. One condition for having the right to a meaningful opinion is that one has internalized the structures of discourse that make the artworld an institutional reality. Not all critics, nor all collectors or dealers, nor all artists at a given time need be part of the artworld, so there is only a partial intersection of this institution and the other institutions of art. Still, it is what makes for the possibility of there being an *avant-garde* or what journalists refer to these days as a "cutting edge."

What was, I think, particularly brilliant about that page in *Life* was the interaction it set up with its readers, demanding and making inevitable a response of some kind, provoking the reader to participate in an incipient artworld. The arguments and discussions the magazine may have generated among readers—"Can you imagine . . . The greatest living artist! . . . It looks like my cat peed against the canvas . . . Art? How? . . . "—drew them into an artworld-like relationship with one another. Of course *Life* did not take the reader very far into the kinds of issues that would have nourished rational debate; the impulses of *People* magazine and of the trivia craze to come are inscribed already in the text of 1949. Still, when one thinks of media and the arts, the *Life* story comes forward for its powerful role of engagement with its readers, setting up between reader and text the beginning of a discussion which, with more information, begins to constitute the being and the value of the work.

That's a tiny compliment, and the problem remains how far this discussion could have gotten when most *Life* readers in 1949 were restricted to the puzzling images of the work, the almost comical images of the artist, and the snide and supercilious text they illustrated. Had it been our era of mass television, one can imagine—after the top stories, the sports and weather, and the break for "these important messages"—images of a tense, crouching Pollock, swinging his dripping paint stick across a canvas on the floor, followed by a close-up of Greenberg, bald, aggressive, sarcastic, speaking in the nasal accents of the New York intellectual above the words "Clement Greenberg, Critic," saying, "Yes, Pat, Pollock is the towering genius of the scene, the greatest painter to have come along in the history of this country." And then Pat faces the viewers and gives us two 900 numbers to phone in our vote on the question, "Is he the greatest living painter in the United States?" What would such a vote mean, what rights have we to an opinion if all we have to go on are those images and the views of "the expert"?

In a somewhat disobliging discussion of the Institutional Theory of Art in his magisterial work *Painting as an Art*, the philosopher Richard Wollheim calls into question the idea of authority as the property of formidable East Coast or other highbrows. He uses to this end an argument first made by Plato to issue from the mouth of Socrates in the great dialogue *The Euthyphro*. Euthyphro advertises himself as an expert on matters of piety, which he defines as what the gods all love. Do they love it because it is piety, Socrates slyly asks, or is it piety only because they love it? The gods may indeed be authoritative on questions of what they love, and if piety is merely that, then the gods are themselves authoritative on piety. But if they love it because it is piety, then there is a distinction between piety and what they love, and the question can be put of the grounds on which they recognize piety when they encounter it. And this makes the fact that the gods love piety irrelevant to the nature of piety, which is a matter of what those grounds are. We can learn what those grounds are and get to be as expert as the gods. So with art. If art is just what the highbrow experts love, that gives them only the authority to say what they love, not why it is great. If they love it because it is art, or is great art, then the grounds must be independent of their feelings, and all we have to know are those grounds: The artworld is as irrelevant as the gods.

This was a good argument in Plato's time, and it is a good argument today. The point, however, is that one gets to be a member of the artworld by coming to understand what the grounds are for saying that something is art, or good art, or great art. It is a reason-giving activity, to participate in the artworld, and though in the end one may acquire taste, taste itself is something that is trained, refined and developed. So one has to participate in the arguments of the artworld in order to have a view that counts for anything. When I saw that piece in *Life*, I realized, like Socrates, that I knew nothing at all about the art of the present moment, despite having tramped since childhood through the silent galleries of the Detroit Institute of Art, including those rarely visited upstairs rooms where one could see Matisse and the German expressionists. So I began to read Greenberg, got familiar, in a distant way, with some of the artists, listened to the endless arguments, and saw what Pollock had done. And when I wrote my piece in *The Journal of Philosophy,* I believed that I had witnessed the decline of one whole complex of reasons and beliefs and the emergence of another whole complex, which led me to reflect on the shape of historical change in art—not only on the philosophical issues raised by Warhol's Brillo boxes, but on the fact that unless one was prepared to take a reasoned philosophical stand there would be no way of seeing why the Brillo boxes meant anything or even what the conditions are for something to have meaning as an artwork.

It was a different world in those days. Ordinary persons, even if quite cultivated, did not cross the thresholds of art galleries, much as men do not commonly cross those of lingerie shops. One would not know what the proper behavior was, what questions to ask, what answers to give if there were questions. Even in 1964 the artworld was encapsulated in the wider society, whose knowledge, such as it was, was transmitted in pieces not much better (probably much worse) than *Life* in 1949. There doubtless was a general belief, tacitly held, that on balance it was good that there were artists making art, without anyone being able to say how or why it was good. People in other societies might similarly feel that it was on the whole a good thing that there were enclaves in which religious devotions were being practiced by those called to them, though no one could say exactly how that good came about. Moreover, art did little harm. It would have been a matter of general indifference that people who cared about such things would spend good money acquiring what one would not be caught dead having in one's basement, woodshed, attic or garage. Art was a private matter for consenting adults, the kind of stuff one's wife dragged one off to see on trips to Paris and London. This situation prevailed through the '60s and into the '70s. Pollock was a kind of star, Warhol a kind of superstar. But who knew Franz Kline or Robert Motherwell, Mark Rothko or Barnett Newman? Who knew Claes Oldenberg and James Rosenquist, Robert Rauschenberg and Jasper Johns?

And then all this changed. I don't know how to explain the change, nor do I know if the media caused or only reflected it, but in the 1980s art became a public matter. More and more people, if not precisely enfranchised into the artworld, attended more and more exhibitions as the local museum grew into the defining social center of the contemporary community. Beyond the gift shop and the cafeteria, there were educational programs, special exhibitions, lecture series. People paid admissions, became members, joined committees and attended exhibitions that in an earlier decade would have been the purview only of those with very advanced tastes. More and more people wanted to study to become artists, more curators and administrators were trained to run the increasing number of museums—and the media, by and large, responded in kind. Art critics were hired, who were in general as well informed about their beats as sportswriters were about theirs, and kept track of the main shows in New York, Paris and London, interviewing artists as they came through, writing up the exhibited new acquisitions for increasingly interested readers. It was an extension of the largely benevolent attitude toward art of the previous decades, together with this increased sophistication, that the arts should become something publicly funded—that there should be public art, as well as public subsidies for the making of private art and for its display. And suddenly, like a harsh confirmation of the dialectical view of history, art suddenly bit the hand that fed it, and moved, in the mass media, from the arts and leisure section to the front page and the editorial page. Suddenly, in the 1980s, art impinged upon the wider political consciousness in ways that engaged the deepest values of the society. And engaged them in ways that were not remediable through learning the rules of the artworld. The public was entrapped in discussions of its basic conceptions of human rights and moral values.

The two major collisions of the decade were, of course, the Corcoran's decision to cancel an exhibition of the photography of Robert Mapplethorpe in order to forestall congressional anger—which it instead succeeded in arousing—and the decision of the Human Services Administration to remove Richard Serra's "Tilted Arc" from the public space it had been commissioned for on grounds that it deprived users of that space of the freedom to enjoy it. These were very different cases to be sure, but each could be presented to the public in such a way that it would be perfectly legitimate to call in your opinion to the convenient 900 number. Art was complicated maybe, but no more so than most of what we are asked to cast our votes on. These were issues which citizens in their capacity as citizens were entitled to vote on, however much or little they knew about art. Expertise counted for very little.

In the "Tilted Arc" hearings the artworld drew its wagons into a circle and united in saying that Serra was extremely gifted, that "Tilted Arc" was a site-specific artwork and beautifully suited to its purposes. None of this counted. The artworld could be authoritative on these issues without that authority extending to the question of whether the work should be removed. At the borderline between art and life the artworld faces the rest of life, and it has to learn to explain, to educate, to lobby like any other interested group in order to get its way by means of the consent of those affected. The artworld failed to do this, and "Tilted Arc" fell. (In a similar instance, the Whitney Museum failed to do this with its architectural plans for a new museum addition and the building failed to rise.)

The Mapplethorpe case was of a kind that could not have earned a page in *Life* like Pollock's. The very nature of the controversy precluded publishing "Man in a Polyester Suit" accompanied by a picture of the dandyish Mapplethorpe and the question, "Is this the greatest living photographer in the United States?" If a mass media publication could have carried that image—a black, suited figure with an elephantine penis hanging heavily through his fly—there would have been no controversy. In the Whitney exhibition of Mapplethorpe's work, which preceded the Corcoran cancellation, the museum could not even get the printer of its catalog to include the photographer's image of a young girl with her legs spread apart. Mapplethorpe's erotic works were pretty rough even for the artworld, and many raised the question of whether they were art at all. But in this the artworld only reproduced the controversy between itself and the wider society, which was suddenly concerned that its taxes were being spent on work like this, or on Andres Serrano's "Piss Christ."

Roberta Smith, one of the *New York Time*'s best critics, raised the question of whether these images were art in the context of a wider discussion that asked the same question about some paintings of David Hockney and some glassworks of Dale Chihuly. She did this before the Corcoran fiasco, just after the Mapplethorpe show at the Whitney had closed (it had hardly caused a ripple in New York, when it was up). She did so as a member of the artworld, raising once more the definition of art, saying in effect that maybe there are limits. Whether it is art, like the questions raised in "The Artworld" in 1964, is something to be worked through by reasoned argument. You could not show the offending Mapplethorpes on CNN, but even if you could the question of whether they are art would not be a matter of counting votes on the 900 number. On the other hand, the question of whether to spend public money on work that many find morally offensive is a 900–number question. It is an issue for the editorial page and the news page, not the arts and leisure section. The media has come a long way since *Life* in 1949, but that's because art has come a long way and society has come a long way, with the media the mirror of their mingling.

Arthur C. Danto is Johnsonian Professor Emeritus of Philosophy at Columbia University and art critic for The Nation. *This chapter originally appeared in the winter 1990* Media Studies Journal, *"Arts & Media."*

10

A Decade of Change

Compiled by Jennifer Kelley

Freedom Forum Media Studies Center dialogue and *Media Studies Journal* interviews with scholars, commentators and media professionals identified these critical trends and events in the media.

1. Media industry mergers accompanied by the compression of ownership and the growth in management of journalism organizations by nonjournalists.
2. Fragmentation of the media audience spurred by the decline of traditional broadcast networks and general-interest magazines and the growth of cable television and special-interest media.
3. Interactive, computerized media technology for a narrow audience, presenting economic and technological challenges to advertiser-supported mass media such as broadcasting.
4. A movement away from local media serving an audience in a small geographic area and toward nationally oriented media organized to serve demographically defined markets irrespective of geography.
5. An institutional struggle to set social and political agendas, embroiling media, government and market forces.
6. A continuing decline of faith in public institutions, especially the media and government.
7. Debates over the composition of the media workforce—especially with regard to race, ethnicity and gender—and its relationship to news coverage.
8. A nagging public criticism that the news media are dominated by amoral, market-driven owners and biased reporters.

9. The rise of media formats that blur the distinction between entertainment and news. While some major newspapers and television networks let tabloids set the agenda for political coverage, others begin a debate over their mission and standards.
10. An impasse in discussions of the media's shortcomings defined by the near-reflexive invocation of the First Amendment to defend any practice and an equally facile appeal to the market as the solution to every problem.

Journalism and Its Public

WALTER CRONKITE: My feeling is that journalism generally—and I do emphasize generally—has improved over the years from the highly personalized editorial-type journalism from the last century and the early parts of this century through the rather wildly tabloid-type journalism and somewhat nonintellectual journalism of the period up to World War II, a journalism that was practiced for the most part by only moderately well-educated people. College degrees were hardly required for newspaper reporters and rewrite men and copy editors in those days. From those days to today there's been considerable improvement. After World War II the requirement of a college degree became almost standard for most newspapers, and today many of the larger newspapers seek graduate degrees as well. So we've got a body of better-educated reporters, writers and editors than we ever have before, and I think that the influence of that is seen in the papers. I think for the most part the stories are better written and better reported.

The problem today is that television has brought a destabilizing influence into journalism. In broadcasting itself, the time requirement is so restrictive it has led to a distortion through pressure in a sense—the pressure of trying to fit a maximum amount of information into a minimum amount of time. And the networks and the others have not provided enough time for a thorough explanation of breaking stories, so that people are living by headlines. This, as well as the entire change in our environment today, the speeded-up lifestyle of the American people (and indeed people all around the world) is such that the newspapers have found it necessary to try to copy something of the television style, and there is a hypercompression it seems to me in a lot of reporting at a lot of newspapers.

I find the columns frequently found on second pages of newspapers today briefing the news in one paragraph to a story simply an insidious copy of what you get on television, and I'm afraid a lot of people are just reading that and hardly indulging in the longer stories that the papers do provide. Along with that, there's been an attempt on the part of a lot of the newspapers to entertain—to hold their readers by a features approach to so much of the news. It seems to me this creates a deterioration of the serious approach to the news that I feel the newspapers ought to have. It's getting more and more difficult today to go to a source where you can just get the facts laid out in front of you—the who, what, when, where, why and how of old-fashioned journalism—and be sure that it's all there and done as objectively and fairly as journalism can do it. I see too much attempt to "featurize," which means bringing in a lot of adjectives that are in most cases personal opinion. That disturbs me.

I don't decry the reporting of the aberrant behavior of our fellow citizens. I think the O.J. Simpson case, which is so much in the discussion among journalists today, is a perfectly valid news story. It's got some fascinating characters and some fascinating subplots, and therefore it is a good news story. It is being vastly overplayed to my mind. I can't believe that the public is really hanging on every one of these minor developments in the pretrial proceedings. But it's a legitimate news story; I accept that.

I can't accept the crass commercialization of the news—the purchasing of interviews. People are paying for interviews today, and how can the public trust for one minute people who are concocting, perhaps, stories in order to get the highest bid? I just can't understand how we can accept this at all.

I don't think the readers and viewers *en masse* are as well read and as well tutored in the news as they used to be. I think when they depended more on the newspaper, and in the leisure they used to have at home at night, instead of all the divertissements for their time today, that they read better and read more and read more carefully than they do today. The fact is, as we know, that the percentage of people getting most of their news from television today is way up there toward the high 80s somewhere, and the people getting all their news from television is more than half of those. And that means that most of the people are not getting enough information to intelligently exercise their franchise, and this is a great danger to the democracy. I am very much concerned about it.

Walter Cronkite is a CBS special correspondent, chairman of Cronkite Ward &Co. and a member of the Media Studies Center's National Advisory Committee.

"It's Demographics, Stupid!"

KEN AULETTA: There is a growing preoccupation, which started in television and has now spread, with chasing younger viewers and readers. As the major media lose audience to specialized publications and new upstart media, institutions that once saw themselves, comfortably, as upholders of a public trust, now panic. So they chase after ratings or circulation, strain to compete with tabloid TV by making network news "more human," strain to compete with the emotion imparted by TV by making print stories more feature oriented, softer, more anecdotal, more opinionated.

Ken Auletta is an author and New Yorker *columnist.*

The Business of News

ALEX JONES: The communications business began as the news business, with people spending money for information. News organizations were usually owned and run by journalists, for whom profit was modest. The news attracted an audience, and that audience attracted advertising. With advertising, eventually, came handsome profit margins.

Over time, the tail of the news business began to wag the dog. While profits had once been in the service of news, news came to be a means to profits at many news organizations. When profit margins were jeopardized by hard times, news was sacrificed.

But even so, the essential nature of the communications industry's corporate culture has remained one where judgments were made by people who had some journalistic knowledge and sense of pride or obligation under the First Amendment. At some level, those running communications companies usually think of themselves as journalists.

That is changing.

As ownership of the nation's communications industry becomes more and more consolidated, many of those enterprises doing the acquiring are noncommunications companies run by people who have no sense of journalistic mission, responsibility or tradition. They have other priorities. Yet they will control most of the nation's journalism.

That is very dangerous.

Alex Jones is an author and host of WNYC's radio show "On the Media."

A Loss of Leaders

ROBERT SCHULMAN: Over this last decade, we have been losing tremendous leadership voices in the news business, in journalism. Who speaks commandingly now on behalf of most of the press? Who has that respect that individuals of past decades used to be able to attract? Maybe this is the voice of an over-age destroyer speaking, but we had the Tom Winships and the Otis Chandlers and indeed, going way back, the A.J. Lieblings. Who is there now that can attract that kind of clarion call respect? I feel that it is a significant concern and a significant loss. In broadcast we used to have Ed Murrow, who had more warts and shortcomings than were generally recognized, but when he spoke he commanded attention. Later his old associate, Fred Friendly. And, for all of his showboater tendencies, you had a Ben Bradlee. Now he's confused with Jason Robards. This is not to detract from the skill or the professionalism of some of the people now in catbird seat positions in the news media, but somehow they don't have the acceptability that makes them immediately noted for what they say.

Robert Schulman, veteran journalist and media critic, is executive director of the Center for Humanities/Civic Leadership at the University of Louisville.

The Media and Race

JANNETTE L. DATES: I'm worried about the trend of polarization between black and white people in this country. There was a time when it seemed that we were coming together, that the experiment called democracy would work out. But the assassinations in the '60s set off a downward spiral and we're still in it. People are afraid of standing up and forging alliances. They are sticking with 'my group.' It takes a lot of courage to reach out. Most people are sticking to I, me and mine. The media plays to this. If you look at films, they usually diminish or demean the presence of African Americans or other different groups in some way. In the movie industry, negative characters are used to stereotype black people. Violence and despair are the traits put forward by Hollywood as defining characteristics of black communities. But if that were true none of us would have made it out of the ghetto and into the middle class, and there is a burgeoning black middle class.

Jannette L. Dates is an author and acting dean of the School of Communications at Howard University.

II

The Media, Politics and Policy

11

Journalism, Publicity and the
Lost Art of Argument

Christopher Lasch

Let us begin with a simple proposition: What democracy requires is public debate, not information. Of course it needs information, too, but the kind of information it needs can be generated only by vigorous popular debate. We do not know what we need to know until we ask the right questions, and we can identify the right questions only by subjecting our own ideas about the world to the test of public controversy. Information, usually seen as the precondition of debate, is better understood as its by-product. When we get into arguments that focus and fully engage our attention, we become avid seekers of relevant information. Otherwise we take in information passively—if we take it in at all.

From these considerations it follows that the job of the press is to encourage debate, not to supply the public with information. But as things now stand the press generates information in abundance, and nobody pays any attention. It is no secret that the public knows less about public affairs than it used to know. Millions of Americans cannot begin to tell you what is in the Bill of Rights, what Congress does, what the Constitution says about the powers of the presidency, how the party system emerged or how it operates. A sizable majority, according to a recent survey, believe that Israel is an Arab nation. Ignorance of public affairs is commonly attributed to the failure of the public schools, and only secondarily to the failure of the press to inform. But since the public no longer participates in debates on national issues, it has no reason to be better informed. When debate becomes a lost art, information makes no impression.

Though the question at first may seem to have little to do with the issues raised by modern publicity, let us ask why debate has become a lost art. The answer may surprise: Debate began to decline around the turn of the century, when the press became more "responsible," more professional, more conscious of its civic obligations. In the early 19th century the press was fiercely partisan. Until the middle of the century, papers were often financed by political parties. Even when they became more independent of parties, they did not embrace the ideal of objectivity or neutrality. In 1841 Horace Greeley launched his *New York Tribune* with the announcement that it would be a "journal removed alike from servile partisanship on the one hand and from gagged, mincing neutrality on the other." Strong-minded editors like Greeley, James Gordon Bennett, E.L. Godkin and Samuel Bowles objected to the way in which the demands of party loyalty infringed upon editorial independence, making the editor merely a mouthpiece for a party or faction; but they did not attempt to conceal their own views or to impose a strict separation of news and editorial content. Their papers were journals of opinion in which the reader expected to find a definite point of view, together with unrelenting criticism of opposing points of view.

It is no accident that journalism of this kind flourished during the period from 1830 to 1900, when popular participation in politics was at its height. Eighty percent of the eligible voters typically went to the polls in presidential elections. After 1900 the percentage declined sharply (65 percent in 1904 and 59 percent in 1912), and it has continued to decline more or less steadily throughout the 20th century. Torchlight parades, mass rallies and gladiatorial contests of oratory made 19th-century politics an object of consuming popular interest. Horace Mann's account of the campaign of 1848 conveys something of the vitality of 19th-century politics, all the more impressive when we remember that this particular account came from someone who be-

lieved that the attention devoted to politics might better have been
devoted to education:

> Agitation pervaded the country. There was no stagnant mind; there was no stag-
> nant atmosphere. . . . Wit, argument, eloquence, were in such demand, that they
> were sent for at the distance of a thousand miles—from one side of the Union to
> the other. The excitement reached the humblest walks of life. The mechanic in his
> shop made his hammer chime to the music of political rhymes; and the farmer, as
> he gathered in his harvest, watched the aspects of the political, more vigilantly
> than of the natural, sky. Meetings were everywhere held. . . . The press showered
> its sheets over the land, thick as snow-flakes in a wintry storm. Public and private
> histories were ransacked, to find proofs of honor or proofs of dishonor; political
> economy was invoked; the sacred names of patriotism, philanthropy, duty to God,
> and duty to man, were on every tongue.

Mann's account suggests that 19th-century journalism served as an
extension of the town meeting. It created a public forum in which the
issues of the day were hotly debated. Newspapers not only reported
political controversies but participated in them, drawing in their readers as well. Print culture rested on the remnants of an oral tradition.
Print was not yet the exclusive medium of communication, nor had it
severed its connection with spoken language. The printed language
was still shaped by the rhythms and requirements of the spoken word,
in particular by the conventions of verbal argumentation. Print served
to create a larger forum for the spoken word, not yet to displace or
reshape it.

The "best men," as they liked to think of themselves, were never
altogether happy with this state of affairs. Horace Mann, even though
he was himself elected to Congress in the 1848 election, regarded
party strife as the bane of the republic. In his view, education belonged exclusively in schools; it did not occur to him that public
controversy might be educational in its own right. Because it divided
men instead of bringing them together, he believed, public controversy
was something to be avoided. The political wars, moreover, usually
ended in the victory of demagogues and spoilsmen, not of the "best
men."

By the 1870s and 1880s, Mann's low opinion of politics had come
to be widely shared by the educated classes. The scandals of the Gilded
Age gave party politics a bad name. Genteel reformers —"mugwumps,"
to their enemies—demanded a professionalization of politics, designed
to free the civil service from party control and to replace political

appointees with trained experts. Even those who rejected the invitation to declare their independence from the party system, like Theodore Roosevelt (whose refusal to desert the Republican Party infuriated the "independents"), shared the enthusiasm for civil service reform. The "best men" ought to challenge the spoilsmen on their own turf, according to Roosevelt, instead of retreating to the sidelines of political life.

The drive to clean up politics gained momentum in the Progressive era. Under the leadership of Roosevelt, Woodrow Wilson, Robert La Follette and William Jennings Bryan, the Progressives preached "efficiency," "good government," "bipartisanship" and the "scientific management" of public affairs, and declared war on "bossism." They attacked the seniority system in Congress, limited the powers of the speaker of the House, replaced mayors with city managers, and delegated important governmental functions to appointive commissions staffed with trained administrators. Recognizing that political machines were welfare agencies of a rudimentary type, which dispensed jobs and other benefits to their constituents and thereby won their loyalty, the Progressives set out to create a welfare state as a way of competing with the machines. They launched comprehensive investigations of crime, vice, poverty and other "social problems." They took the position that government was a science, not an art. They forged links between government and the university so as to assure a steady supply of experts and expert knowledge. On the other hand, they had little use for public debate. Most political questions were too complex, in their view, to be submitted to popular judgment. They liked to contrast the scientific expert with the orator—the latter a useless windbag whose rantings only confused the public mind.

Professionalism in politics meant professionalism in journalism. The connection between them was spelled out by Walter Lippmann in a notable series of books: *Liberty and the News* (1920), *Public Opinion* (1922) and *The Phantom Public* (1925). These provided a founding charter for modern journalism—the most elaborate rationale for a journalism guided by the new ideal of professional objectivity. Lippmann held up standards by which the press is still judged—usually with the result that it is found wanting.

What concerns us here, however, is not whether the press has lived up to Lippmann's standards but how he arrived at those standards in the first place and what their connection to advertising and public relations is today. In 1920 Lippmann and Charles Merz published a long essay in *The New Republic* examining press coverage of the Russian Revolution. This study, now forgotten, showed that American papers gave their readers an account of the revolution distorted by anti-Bolshevik prejudices, wishful thinking and sheer ignorance. *Liberty and the News* was also prompted by the collapse of journalistic objectivity during the war, when the newspapers had appointed themselves "defenders of the faith." The result, according to Lippmann, was a "breakdown of the means of public knowledge." The difficulty went beyond war or revolution, the "supreme destroyers of realistic thinking." The traffic in sex, violence and "human interest"—staples of modern mass journalism —raised grave questions about the future of democracy. "All that the sharpest critics of democracy have alleged is true if there is no steady supply of trustworthy and relevant news."

In *Public Opinion* and *The Phantom Public*, Lippmann answered the critics, in effect, by redefining democracy. Democracy did not require that the people literally govern themselves. The public's stake in government was strictly procedural. The public interest did not extend to the substance of decision-making: "The public is interested in law, not in the laws; in the method of law, not in the substance." Questions of substance should be decided by knowledgeable administrators whose access to reliable information immunized them against the emotional "symbols" and "stereotypes" that dominated public debate. The public was incompetent to govern itself and did not even care to do so, in Lippmann's view. But as long as rules of fair play were enforced, the public would be content to leave government to experts—provided, of course, that the experts delivered the goods, the ever-increasing abundance of comforts and conveniences so closely identified with the American way of life.

Lippmann acknowledged the conflict between his recommendations and the received theory of democracy, according to which citizens ought to participate in discussions of public policy and to have a hand, if only indirectly, in decision-making. Democratic theory, he argued, had its roots in social conditions that no longer obtained. It presupposed an "omnicompetent citizen," a "jack of all trades" who could be found only in a "simple self-contained community." In the "wide and unpredictable environment" of the modern world, the old ideal of citizenship was obsolete. A complex industrial society required a government carried on by officials who would necessarily be guided—since any form of direct democracy was now impossible—either by public opinion or by expert knowledge. Public opinion was unreliable because it could be united only by an appeal to slogans and "symbolic pictures." Lippmann's distrust of public opinion rested on the epistemological distinction between truth and mere opinion. Truth, as he conceived it, grew out of disinterested scientific inquiry; everything else was ideology. The scope of public debate, accordingly, had to be severely restricted. At best, public debate was a disagreeable necessity—not the very essence of democracy but its "primary defect," which arose only because "exact knowledge," unfortunately, was in limited supply. Ideally, public debate would not take place at all; decisions would be based on scientific "standards of measurement" alone. Science cut through "entangling stereotypes and slogans," the "threads of memory and emotion" that kept the "responsible administrator" tied up in knots.

The role of the press, as Lippmann saw it, was to circulate information, not to encourage argument. The relationship between information and argument was antagonistic, not complementary. He did not take the position that reliable information was a necessary precondition of argument; on the contrary, his point was that information precluded argument, made argument unnecessary. Arguments were what took place in the absence of reliable information. Lippmann had forgotten what he learned (or should have learned) from William James and John Dewey: that our search for reliable information is itself guided by the questions that arise during arguments about a given course of action. It is only by subjecting our preferences and projects to the test of debate that we come to understand what we know and what we still need to learn. Until we have to defend our opinions in public, they remain opinions in Lippmann's pejorative sense—half-formed convictions based on random impressions and unexamined assumptions. It is the act of articulating and defending our views that lifts them out of the category of "opinions," gives them shape and definition, and makes it possible for others to recognize them as a description of their own experience as well. In short, we come to know our own minds only by explaining ourselves to others.

The attempt to bring others around to our own point of view carries the risk, of course, that we may adopt their point of view instead. We have to enter imaginatively into our opponents' arguments, if only for the purpose of refuting them, and we may end up being persuaded by those we sought to persuade. Argument is risky and unpredictable— and therefore educational. Most of us tend to think of it (as Lippmann thought of it) as a clash of rival dogmas, a shouting match in which neither side gives any ground. But arguments are not won by shouting down opponents. They are won by changing opponents' minds—something that can happen only if we give opposing arguments a respectful hearing and still persuade their advocates that there is something wrong with those arguments. In the course of this activity, we may well decide that there is something wrong with our own.

If we insist on argument as the essence of education, we will defend democracy not as the most efficient but as the most educational form of government—one that extends the circle of debate as widely as possible and thus forces all citizens to articulate their views, to put their views at risk and to cultivate the virtues of eloquence, clarity of thought and expression, and sound judgment. As Lippmann noted, small communities are the classic locus of democracy—not because they are "self-contained," however, but simply because they allow everyone to take part in public debates. Instead of dismissing direct democracy as irrelevant to modern conditions, we need to recreate it on a large scale. And from this point of view, the press serves as the equivalent of the town meeting.

This is what Dewey argued, in effect—though not, unfortunately, very clearly—in *The Public and Its Problems* (1927), a book written in reply to Lippmann's disparaging studies of public opinion. Lippmann's distinction between truth and information rested on a "spectator theory of knowledge," as James W. Carey explains in his *Communication as Culture* (1988). As Lippmann understood these matters, knowledge is what we get when an observer, preferably a scientifically trained observer, provides us with a copy of reality that we can all recognize. Dewey, on the other hand, knew that even scientists argue among themselves. "Systematic inquiry," he contended, was only the beginning of knowledge, not its final form. The knowledge needed by any community—whether it is a community of scientific inquirers or a political community—emerges only from "dialogue" and "direct give and take."

It is significant, as Carey points out, that Dewey's analysis of communication stressed the ear rather than the eye. "Conversation," Dewey wrote, "has a vital import lacking in the fixed and frozen words of written speech. . . . The connections of the ear with vital and out-going thought and emotion are immensely closer and more varied than those of the eye. Vision is a spectator; hearing is a participator."

The press extends the scope of debate by supplementing the spoken word with the written word. If the press needs to apologize for anything, it is not that the written word is a poor substitute for the pure language of mathematics. What matters, in this connection, is that the written word is a poor substitute for the spoken word. It is an acceptable substitute, however, as long as written speech takes spoken speech and not mathematics as its model. According to Lippmann, the press was unreliable because it could never give us accurate representations of reality, only "symbolic pictures" and stereotypes. Dewey's analysis implied a more penetrating line of criticism. As Carey puts it, "The press, by seeing its role as that of informing the public, abandons its role as an agency for carrying on the conversation of our culture." Having embraced Lippmann's ideal of objectivity, the press no longer serves to cultivate "certain vital habits" in the community—"the ability to follow an argument, grasp the point of view of another, expand the boundaries of understanding, debate the alternative purposes that might be pursued."

The rise of the advertising and public relations industries, side by side, helps to explain why the press abdicated its most important function—enlarging the public forum—at the same time that it became more "responsible." A responsible press, as opposed to a partisan or opinionated one, attracted the kind of readers advertisers were eager to reach: well-heeled readers, most of whom probably thought of themselves as independent voters. These readers wanted to be assured that they were reading all the news that was fit to print, not an editor's idiosyncratic and no doubt biased view of things. Responsibility came to be equated with the avoidance of controversy because advertisers were willing to pay for it. Some advertisers were also willing to pay for sensationalism, though on the whole they preferred a respectable readership to sheer numbers. What they clearly did not prefer was "opinion"—not because they were impressed with Lippmann's philosophical arguments but because opinionated reporting did not guarantee the right audience. No doubt they also hoped that an aura of objectivity, the hallmark of responsible journalism, would also rub off on the advertisements that surrounded increasingly slender columns of print.

In a curious historical twist, advertising, publicity and other forms of commercial persuasion themselves came to be disguised as information. Advertising and publicity substituted for open debate. "Hidden persuaders" (as Vance Packard called them) replaced the old-time editors, essayists and orators who made no secret of their partisanship. And information and publicity became increasingly indistinguishable. Most of the "news" in our newspapers—40 percent, according to the conservative estimate of Professor Scott Cutlip of the University of Georgia—consists of items churned out by press agencies and public relations bureaus and then regurgitated intact by the "objective" organs of journalism. We have grown accustomed to the idea that most of the space in newspapers, so called, is devoted to advertising—at least two-thirds in most newspapers. But if we consider public relations as another form of advertising, which is hardly farfetched since private, commercially inspired enterprises fuel both, we now have to get used to the idea that much of the "news" consists of advertising, too.

The decline of partisan press and the rise of a new type of journalism professing rigorous standards of objectivity do not assure a steady supply of usable information. Unless information is generated by sustained public debate, most of it will be irrelevant at best, misleading and manipulative at worst. Increasingly, information is generated by those who wish to promote something or someone—a product, a cause, a political candidate or officeholder—without arguing their case on its merits or explicitly advertising it as self-interested material either. Much of the press, in its eagerness to inform the public, has become a conduit for the equivalent of junk mail. Like the post office—another institution that once served to extend the sphere of face-to-face discussion and to create "committees of correspondence" —it now delivers an abundance of useless, indigestible information that nobody wants, most of which ends up as unread waste. The most important effect of this obsession with information, aside from the destruction of trees for paper and the mounting burden of "waste management," is to undermine the authority of the word. When words are used merely as instruments of publicity or propaganda, they lose their power to persuade. Soon they cease to mean anything at all. People lose the capacity to use language precisely and expressively, or even to distinguish one word from another. The spoken word models itself on the written word instead of the other way around, and ordinary speech begins to sound like the clotted jargon we see in print. Ordinary speech begins to sound like "information"—a disaster from which the English language may never recover.

Christopher Lasch, who died in 1994, was Don Alonzo Watson Professor of History at the University of Rochester and author of many books, including The Culture of Narcissism. *This chapter originally appeared in the spring 1990* Media Studies Journal, *"Publicity."*

12

Bystanders as Opinion Makers—
A Bottoms-Up Perspective

Herbert J. Gans

The conventional wisdom about public opinion has it shaped largely by opinion makers—by the politicians and other persuaders. Pundits, the latter are sometimes called. These include columnists, commentators, experts, lobbyists, spin directors and flacks, but sometimes also celebrities, entertainers, advertisers—and even academics. Undoubtedly pundits play a significant role in producing the topical opinions that are now instantly needed after major news events. Opinion makers also introduce some ideas into the long-term, less rapidly changing public opinion that reflects the country's dominant political attitudes and values.

Nonetheless, the prime controllers of long-term public opinion, the people who dispose over it and propose more of it than the conventional wisdom gives them credit for, are the Americans I call bystanders. These are the normally politically uninvolved members of the general public, and altogether they constitute the vast majority of that public. Politicians have them in mind when they refer to "the American people."

In addition, bystanders frequently have a significant role in making topical opinion. They may not feel deeply about the latest *coup d'état* in a turmoil-ridden country (although they will supply an opinion when primed by a pollster: "As you know, the fourth *coup d'état* in a year recently took place in . . . "). After all, most are opposed to *coups d'état* in principle.

However when current events connect directly to a cherished long-term opinion, bystanders do not need the pollster's aid to offer a topical opinion. In 1987 large numbers of people were opposed to any further military aid to the Contras, and their opinion probably drove the last nail into the Contra coffin. Pundits, educators and geographers were appalled when poll questions showed that majorities knew neither which side "we" were supporting in Nicaragua nor where exactly the country is located, but those particular facts were not needed for an opinion. People did know two more relevant facts: that Nicaragua is small and unlikely to become a security risk for the United States, and that above all they did not want the government involved in any policy that could result in American boys having to fight in Nicaragua.

The belief that the general public has little to do with opinion making and that politicians and pundits do most of it is, among other things, a typical expression of the "top-down" perspective on American society. Its adherents tend to be preoccupied with elites and see rank-and-file Americans only dimly if at all. To be precise, from the top the rank and file look like sheep following the elite opinion makers, but this portrayal is as insulting as it is inaccurate. A "bottoms-up" or "street-level" perspective on society is necessary to understand the indirect and not easily apparent part that bystanders play in making public opinion. Actually, politicians and pundits who aim for a long career in dealing with public opinion quickly develop such a perspective, for they soon learn that they have to figure out what their bystander constituencies will accept, reject, ignore and demand. But then all successful leaders know that they must often be good followers.

In the top-down perspective the news media play a central role. Because people are thought to be essentially passive, the news media are viewed not only as transmitting information but also imposing the agendas of politicians, pundits and even journalists on news audiences. The bottoms-up angle of vision on society assigns a far lesser role to the news media. It assumes that people choose what they wish to consider from what they watch or read but make up their minds—

and develop opinions—on the basis of many other considerations. Indeed, a bottoms-up approach observes that because the news media need to attract large audiences, these audiences also help to set the agenda for the news media. Obviously they cannot set the agenda for specific news events, but they give news organizations signals, through ratings and circulations, about which events they prefer to see covered, how they should be covered and how they should be translated into news stories. Journalists are only partially guided by such signals, but they cannot ignore them without turning off some audience members or losing them to competitors.

America's bystanders are hardly a homogeneous population; nor are they the so-called mass public of poor, blue-collar and white-collar people. Instead they come from all strata and sectors of American society, from college-educated professionals to the illiterate, from yuppies to senior citizens, and from all races and national backgrounds. Some may have strong opinions on a variety of topical and long-term political issues, but what they all have in common is that they do not express these opinions publicly and are at best marginally involved in the political arena. They may look in by "keeping up with the news," but their lives are centered around their families, jobs, friends, hobbies or combinations of these. They pay at most irregular attention to national and even local political issues, including many elections. Unlike most of the people who will read this article, they do not work in the politics or media industries, are not news buffs and do not know, or even care, who makes the cover of *Newsweek* or *Time* from week to week.

They also do not follow the journalistic pundits to any great extent. According to the Newspaper Advertising Bureau's 1987 national survey of the media audience, 45 percent of the people sampled said "they usually read or look at" "political opinion columns," and just 2 percent said the columns were one of their three favorite items in their newspaper. Local politics and government, mentioned by 69 percent of the sample, was the most often read or looked at political news; it was also the most liked, being the favorite of 14 percent. The favorite newspaper columnist in surveys like this is usually an advice columnist like "Dear Abby," but I imagine that one of the country's most preferred political pundits is Johnny Carson. Indeed, Carson's political commentary and satire at the beginning of his nightly monologue may well be the best single barometer of what the general public thinks about in politics, and perhaps even of what they think.

Bystanders play many roles in shaping public opinion, but four seem to me uppermost. First and most obviously, they are the major creators of long-term public opinion, as well as of the topical opinions they know and care about. Both types of opinion come out of people's political views and other values as these apply to the political, economic and other issues salient to them—but only after informal consultation with family members, friends, co-workers, neighbors and others in the never-ending conversations that make up daily social life. Politicians and pundits have some input into this process, but it would be illusory to exaggerate their importance. After all, bystanders elect politicians, not the other way around.

Accordingly, bystander opinion is something to be wooed, aroused or, when possible, changed by politicians seeking election and re-election, and much of their campaign activity is oriented to pursuing the bystanders even as they talk about offering them leadership. Modern election campaigns devote an immense amount of energy and money to that pursuit, and the campaign strategists who now get much of that money earn renown as experts in wooing, arousing and changing opinion—until they lose an election. In 1988 the Bush strategists, correctly interpreting data from focus groups (presumably made up largely of bystanders) and prepared to hit below the belt, exploited the furloughed Willie Horton while Dukakis' campaign strategists were still listening to their Harvard colleagues.

Once elected, presidents keep after bystander opinion, for example by trying daily to get a lead spot on the network evening television news. They do this not because they want or need to see themselves on television but to remind viewers that they are on the job earning their last or next vote. When President Bush pressed the Senate to make Senator Tower his secretary of defense, it was presumably not because Mr. Tower was considered indispensable but because the White House needed to show the bystander population that Mr. Bush is a strong and determined president—and one loyal to his friends when he thinks they are being unfairly maligned.

Second, bystanders set rough limits on what can and cannot be said and done by public figures on controversial issues, probably more so in the areas of religion and sex than in politics. The average politician running for election must still attend church or synagogue from time to time, preferably with his or her family. Although divorced and gay politicians are now electable in an increasing proportion of the country, I doubt that anyone advocating atheism would have a chance at public office at the national or state level—and I am not sure a syndicated national columnist could keep his or her column after such an announcement. However, national politicians who are militantly fundamentalist are not electable either these days. In politics as in commercial TV, pressure groups and lobbies set limits long before bystanders get around to it, although the power of such groups is enhanced if they can arouse numbers of bystanders to their cause from time to time.

The bystanders' third role is equally indirect. The people who run America's major institutions have enough day-to-day crises to deal with that they want to keep bystanders standing by quietly—and approvingly. As a result, much political activity and rhetoric is framed with this purpose in mind. For example, legislation and governmental budgets are written so that bystanders are positively impressed. As with warranties on new cars, only those with technical expertise or the loyal audiences for investigative reporters and reform-minded columnists find out about the small print. Political decisions that cannot be designed in such fashion are frequently announced on the weekend so that they get into the TV news or newspaper headlines when audiences are at their smallest and least attentive. Even totalitarian governments sometimes work hard to observe democratic formalities in the hope of impressing at least some bystanders. Cover-ups like Watergate are elaborately constructed for exactly the same reason.

Much of what is done to keep bystanders happy takes the form of symbolic politics in which sacred or widely supported cultural and political symbols play a principal role. Congress likes to pass resolutions in support of the American flag, and the Reagan administration described economic policies that enriched the upper class as certain to increase overall economic growth, one of the country's most potent symbols since the age of middle-class affluence ended in the mid-1970s. Symbolic politics is often accompanied by image politics, in which presidential candidates carry their own suitcases and incumbents approve espionage-novel schemes to rescue hostages or invade tiny islands in the Caribbean.

Symbolic and image politics can easily look like posturing, and sometimes Europeans shake their heads over what politicians in the United States do to satisfy bystanders. Perhaps European politics has fewer bystanders, or they matter less because the political parties remain strong, but then some European countries still have monarchies that function in part to keep bystanders happy.

Fourth, at times bystanders are aroused in large numbers and express their opinions directly, and when they do so, politicians and media opinion leaders must learn to follow. Most often, bystanders become visible in local politics when their neighborhoods are threatened by environmental or human enemies that could reduce property and status values, or by today's top issue: the increase in drug-related crime. Occasionally bystanders also make their opinions heard at the national level. In late 1988 the proposal to raise the salaries of the Washington political and judicial elite by 50 percent did the trick—as prior salary increase proposals have frequently done ever since the beginnings of the United States.

On the pay-raise issue, the bystanders not only expressed themselves with near unanimity in the polls, as they had in the past; many were also seen and heard on radio and TV talk shows, which usually stay away from political topics. Those who see society from the top down and perceive bystanders as sheep decided that the opposition to the pay raise was organized by the talk show hosts and would not have materialized without them. In the process they elevated these usually lowly media hosts to at least temporary status as opinion makers. Those who look at society from the bottom up noted that the talk show hosts simply provided an easily accessible outlet for widespread popular discontent—and then promoted it further to raise their ratings. Had the talk shows not suddenly turned into political news programs, the public anger would have found other outlets, for example, a far higher number of calls and letters to elected representatives.

The top-down perspective on public opinion not only produces an inaccurate picture of how American society operates, it also affects the very formation of public opinion. For example, when initial readings of the "public mood" or early measurements of a "public outcry" are needed, politicians and journalists often turn to what editorial writers, columnists, the instant op-ed writers and the experts who appear on television have said—and these are not always true harbingers of how the general public feels. These days public opinion is almost synonymous with polling results, but polls themselves are predominantly top-down affairs. Most of their questions deal with what leading politicians are doing and what issues they are considering, and the main role of poll respondents is to indicate that they "approve/disapprove" or "agree/disagree" with the leaders. In fairness, pollsters also ask different types of questions, but when poll results are turned into news stories these data are often not newsworthy enough to be reported. (The more polls serve as the raw material for news stories, the more pollsters are required to ask questions about the most newsworthy events and the principal newsmakers, and the more poll respondents offer opinions based on the news stories and newsmakers they remember best. Eventually this trend leads to academic studies demonstrating that the news media determine public opinion.)

The bottoms-up approach to public opinion would be far more concerned with what the general public is thinking about. For example, questions about the activities of the country's leaders would have to be followed up by questions about whether people care about the activities, the issues and the leaders themselves—and how much they care. Further questions on why they do or do not care are equally important. Further, bottoms-up questions would then have to ask respondents what issues they care about most—including those not on any public agenda—and what they need most from government, the economy, their employers, and the specific institutions and agencies that impact significantly on their lives. If properly transmitted to and used by politicians, answers to these questions would reduce "inside the Beltway" stereotypes about bystanders and help politicians who want to do so make more democratic decisions. (Of course, politicians must take other leadership factors into account in their decision-making. Even with the best polls, democracy by polling would be undesirable. It would also be unconstitutional.)

Bottoms-up types of questions might also move polling away from the overly impersonal and ritualized exercise that it has become. Standardized items about the country's major problems or the president's ability to handle his job may serve useful news story functions, but they do not allow respondents to express their strongest worries about the country or their deep distrust of most politicians most of the time.

Whether polls are the best measure of public opinion is still debatable, but they cannot properly serve a democratic society until they are reformed in a bottoms-up direction, with questions that cannot be covered by one or two precoded questionnaire items.

Regardless of how public opinion should be measured, politicians know how little effect they normally have on it. So do editorial writers, commentators and other pundits, not to mention lobbyists and public relations experts who are paid to try to change it. All of the above are generally reluctant to publicize the minimal impact they usually have on public opinion—which of course breeds conspiratorial theories of their maximal impact. But the very limitation to their effect on opinion is perhaps the best indicator of the power of bystanders as opinion makers.

Herbert J. Gans is Robert S. Lynd Professor of Sociology at Columbia University and author of several books, including Deciding What's News *and* Middle American Individualism: The Future of Liberal Democracy. *This chapter originally appeared in the spring 1989* Media Studies Journal, *"The Opinion Makers."*

13

Let's Put on a Convention

Reuven Frank

What was new in 1988 was not the recognition that there was no further journalistic purpose in live television coverage of the national political conventions, but that you could say so publicly without being struck by a thunderbolt.

In 1984, when the networks cut back what was widely accepted as the traditional "gavel-to-gavel" coverage to three evening hours each day, the Democratic national committeewoman from the great state of California, among others, got her guaranteed column inches in all the major newspapers by denouncing the "greedy networks."

Networks are indeed greedy, but not uniquely. What is unique about networks is their vulnerability—or at least their self-image as vulnerable. They are big, hulking giants, frightening at first sight, but terrified of mice. They have a race-memory of regulation, license renewal, prosecutorial congressmen and activist commissioners that makes them sweat when confronted by anyone who might conceivably threaten the federally granted license to broadcast. That is why broadcast executives, even broadcast news executives, routinely show up to speak their expensively prepared pieces before congressional subcommittees, whom newspaper publishers, even those with tiny circulations, would not deign to acknowledge (except, perhaps, for a gracious off-the-record lunch, if the chairman asked nicely).

The networks' timidity in the presence of Washington political clout may be the only reason for network convention coverage in 1988. It is hard to find another. Certainly, no one was still bemoaning the passing of "traditional" gavel-to-gavel coverage. There was no gavel-to-gavel convention coverage in radio. It began with television, in Philadelphia in 1948. The TV networks then were skimpy things, a few interconnected cities between Boston and Richmond, nine for NBC, four for ABC, with DuMont and CBS following behind. Most of what the networks spent on television coverage went for sending people and machines to Philadelphia, and organizing them to broadcast from a hall rather than a controlled studio. The actual time on the air, however long or short, added little to the cost. Entertainment programs, on the other hand, cost a lot of money and in those early days earned very little. It saved money to broadcast extra hours from Philadelphia and to shut down the studios in New York, sending home, unpaid, the expensive union electricians, stagehands, musicians and actors. So gavel-to-gavel coverage began with a very traditional purpose: the bottom line (although the term was not yet in wide use). Television cameras panned empty seats while, at each network, the unfortunate reporters who were assigned to "fill" that morning or afternoon droned on about what had happened or what was about to.

Even so, there was novelty, and there was news. Novelty, as Yogi Berra should have said, gets monotonous after a while; but the news took place before our eyes. Candidates were chosen. Some we didn't expect—Estes Kefauver in 1956, William E. Miller in 1964. There were civil rights struggles in platform and credentials committees, even riots in the streets. The conventions were a key step in the distinctive American process of choosing a president.

They no longer are—and that's the point.

News, or the likelihood of news, is what kept the networks covering national political conventions after 1948. Puny, starveling network news departments assumed real status for a few summer weeks out of every 209, and developed a vested interest in going to the conventions to cover them live, controlling the one central, indispensable power in all broadcasting: who gets on the air.

If the conventions of 1948 were seen on television by only a handful of viewers, those of 1952 were a national event. Live television had just gone coast-to-coast. The sale of TV sets skyrocketed in anticipation. Both parties held exciting conventions, and nonfiction television became part of the fabric of American political life. The Republican Party pitted Eisenhower against Taft; in state delegation after state delegation, credentials battles were fought, deciding not only who would be the nominee but who would control the party for the next two decades. The Democrats, in holding the last modern convention to go more than one ballot, switched tracks from Harry Truman to Adlai Stevenson; and the public, glued to its sets, learned that "Democrats always fight." But as regards standards of journalism, and as reporting, the coverage was understaffed and poorly conceived.

In 1956, the pattern of modern convention coverage that still exists was first established. NBC put four skilled reporters on the floor and deployed cameras to follow them as they scoured the delegations looking for news stories—if there were any. The focus shifted forever from podium speeches and anchor booth voiceovers to finding the news and reporting it. CBS and ABC adopted this pattern in 1960, as did CNN in 1984.

All the while, the apparatchiks who run political parties, from county sheriff to United States senator, were becoming increasingly aware that being on television was good for politicians. If a gubernatorial candidate's exposure-intended seconding speech was not being carried, they learned, it was because a municipal chairman was being interviewed by a floor reporter about the barley and oats parity price plank. Either way the politicians could not lose. It was all television; it was all politics; it was all publicity; and it was all wonderful!

Then came one of those inversions so common among American institutions. Politicians stopped thinking about free airtime as their lucky dividend and came to believe that television's purpose for being in the convention hall was to give them exposure. Simultaneously, the evolution of presidential campaigning moved into a new phase. Conventions, which had been inserted into the process more than 150 years ago to take the choosing of candidates away from entrenched oligarchies, gave way to primaries and caucuses, which were perceived as being one step closer to the citizen-voter.

Or—an alternative view of the same evolution—the states instituted primaries and caucuses because they envied the national attention accorded New Hampshire and Wisconsin in the primary process. They looked longingly at the income brought in by the news hordes who stirred their motel martinis with icicles in Dixville Notch. It was a resort town where mostly bellboys voted, but withal the first community to report, in the minutes after midnight of Primary Day, in time for every morning paper in the United States.

No matter how the politicians looked at it, it was still all publicity, and it was still all wonderful!

When the Iowa caucus was inserted to precede the New Hampshire primary, history repeated itself. Estes Kefauver, the junior senator from Tennessee, had made the New Hampshire primary a national news story in 1952. Jimmy Carter, the former governor of Georgia, made the Iowa caucus a national news story in 1976. Both, in their way, moved the focus of attention away from convention time. And the influx of paid employees of news organizations grew—in New Hampshire, in Iowa, in Illinois and Louisiana and California—to approach the number of resident participants, a competitive preening that drove out all other news. How many ways can you misspell "bellwether"?

In this way, the process by which Americans choose their presidents bypassed the national party nominating conventions. And while it is still theoretically possible that no candidate will come through the primary process with a majority of committed delegates, if it did not happen in 1988 it will likely never happen. With nervous optimism, the executives who had to commit network news expenditures last winter and spring anticipated a real fight for the nomination in at least one of the conventions; otherwise, it would be money wasted.

It was money wasted.

The total audience for the three traditional networks' coverage of the 1988 conventions was about 10 percent lower than the total audience in 1984. More telling, in 1988 the conventions on all three networks combined gathered a prime-time rating roughly sufficient to comfortably sustain a prime-time entertainment program on only one of them—in round numbers, a Nielsen rating of about 20.0. This is barely higher than the rating for the first week of NBC's single-network coverage of the 1988 Olympics, which was so disappointing that sponsors had to be mollified with extra "make-good" commercials elsewhere in the schedule.

Need it be said that, these days, money wasted means newspeople fired? Each of the new network proprietors gives his news division a barrel of money. The news division may spend the money, within limits, as it chooses. But when the barrel is empty, that's it. If more is allocated here, less must be allocated there.

News, at the very least, is something that might not have happened. There used to be news in delegates choosing the candidate; there is no longer a choice to make. There used to be news in delegates competing for credentials; elected delegates are now certified by secretaries of state. There used to be news in fights over the party platform; the platform is now decided at another time and in another place. The civil rights struggle and the Vietnam war, the great dramas of recent American history, were played out at the conventions before the cameras. There are no such great dramas these days. There is, in sum, no more news at conventions.

This phenomenon is something far different from the phenomenon of issueless campaigns themselves, which develop no substantial differences between the major candidates and therefore no news (or not the kind of news most voters like to think of as news). Whether or not there are issues in a presidential campaign is a matter of historical context, or accident, or the eye of the beholder. But no news at conventions has become inherent. There can be no news at conventions because conventions do not matter anymore.

Why, then, are they covered? We are, let it be understood, talking here about "covering," not "carrying." News organizations, from all the media, send reporters and editors to spend some of their available time or space with the proceedings at the podium, including the speeches, and the rest to find out what things mean, who is doing what to whom, and how and why the voter is being shortchanged. That is why the networks have floor reporters, and the better-organized networks have reporters covering the more important delegations, sniffing out, tipping off, but never themselves appearing. "Carrying" is something C-SPAN does, interposing no thoughts, questions or independently garnered facts in the presentation not of news of the convention but of the proceedings. This is a noble function, but the distinction must be made.

In the great television news conventions like 1960, 1964 and 1968, the story on the floor among the delegates took over, and the floor reporters were swept along by it. The problem was to make order and sense out of a disorderly landslide of breaking news stories. Twenty years later, on the first day of the 1988 Democratic convention, the floor reporters were asking delegates if they could accept Bentsen as Dukakis' running mate. On the last day, they were still asking the delegates if they could accept Bentsen as Dukakis' running mate. So much trouble to achieve so little needs explaining.

Fear of politicians and the unstated threat of losing the federal license is one explanation for the networks' deployment of enormous, and these days irreplaceable, resources. Inertia is another. Television networks, once they start doing something, find it ridiculously difficult to stop. There is also the pressure inside television news organizations from the Big Mules. The Stars of News like to go to conventions. There they meet old friends and relive old battles, as though they were attending their own conventions. Aspiring news reporters, steeped in the oral tradition, see political conventions as the road to fortune and fame. To be the first to learn whom George Bush would pick as his running mate, NBC's Connie Chung told one newspaper reporter, "can make anyone's career."

Unfortunately for Ms. Chung, another NBC reporter got the story. Unfortunately for every reporter present, that was the only story of the 1988 Republican convention. And unfortunately for the Republican Party, whose leaders, like all politicians, insist on the networks' sacred obligation to cover conventions live, the lack of stories did not dampen the reporters' hunger for news, for airtime, for the Big Prize that can "make anyone's career."

Covering live always develops its own momentum. The three TV networks had about 1,000 news division employees in New Orleans. The juggernaut had to go somewhere, and if Quayle were the only news, it would follow him back to first grade. A perfectly valid story, which would have taken up an hour in 1964, consumed three days in 1988. The people who run the political parties might wish to reconsider how attractive free television exposure is under these conditions. However creatively the story was deflected, the intense concentration on Senator Quayle's past will remain with him and with American politics for a long time. It will also haunt journalism. For the many Americans whose affection for reporters is approaching zero, it was another little nudge.

Three hours a night in 1984. Two hours a night in 1988. In 1992, will there be one hour or none? And if the networks do not cover the conventions, will the parties hold them at all? In 1984, newspaper columnists were challenging network executives and producers to justify shrinking the "traditional" coverage. By 1988, they were fishing for reactions to the ratings. Roone Arledge, the president of ABC News, told *USA Today:* "The two political parties should sit down on their own or maybe with the networks to come up with something more appealing to the American people."

If experience means anything, what might be "more appealing to the American people" would be news, and it is uncomfortable to think of news being made-to-order to help the ratings.

In 1988, as in 1984, the parties enjoyed free television time, but without any news almost nobody watched. The networks, deprived of news, wondered why they should provide free television time. And since the conventions have come to exist only for network television, there will be no conventions if network television does not come. Or will there?

Conventions still have one remaining purpose, a ceremonial one. They ratify; they formalize; they legitimate; they validate. The delegates, chosen in primaries and caucuses, need to gather and to publish their bounden choice. They must dub the candidate who can then go forth to campaign. The meeting will probably be called a national party nominating convention. It will uphold tradition and satisfy continuity.

Like the Electoral College.

Which is not carried on live television.

Reuven Frank created the standard for modern TV convention coverage in 1956. He is a former president of NBC News and author of Out of Thin Air. *This chapter originally appeared in the fall 1988* Media Studies Journal, *"The New Elector."*

14

A Consumer's Guide to Media Truth

Patricia O'Brien

How to advise ordinary people, average "media consumers" (which describes all who read, watch or listen to news), on how to judge if they're getting the Whole Story, or at least a reasonably complete, balanced and fair approximation:

1. "It's just that simple." Sorry, Mr. Perot, it's not, and people should be suspicious when told it is, either by you or the media.

2. Proceed with caution when you hear or read loaded words, the kind that promise more than they deliver. Be wary when somebody "claims" (he's lying), "alleges" (he made it up) or "admits" (he's guilty). Why can't reporters settle for good old "said"? Dull, perhaps, but serviceable and neutral.

3. Beware of the three-facts-make-a-trend story. Trend stories need solid research. Look for the kind of layered reporting that offers both facts and insight before accepting reports of the existence of a trend.

4. Don't swallow any story whole that relies on anonymous quotes or unnamed sources. There's a legitimate struggle on this one, because reporters in search of the truth frequently can't get sources to talk on the record unless they promise anonymity. At the same time, of course,

they leave themselves vulnerable to manipulative political operatives. *Caveat emptor:* Let the media consumer beware.

5. Watch the labels. Does the story purport to be straight, factual news? Is it billed as news analysis? A feature piece? An opinion column or essay? Stories, like grocery products, should be clearly labeled.

6. Learn to identify the cheap shot. One warning sign: The lead is too clever by far. Reporters love a good lead, which is fine, as far as it goes. But having caressed that opener to sparkling perfection, sometimes reporters can't get the rest of the story to deliver on the promise. Other warning signs: If someone's been accused of dire doings, is the charge substantiated, and by whom? (See Point 4, reliance on anonymous sources.) Does the story wrap too neatly? (Refer to Point 1.)

7. Trust your nose. If a story smells bad, it probably is.

8. Learn to recognize the dangers of a news vacuum. Don't let anybody (especially reporters) hurry you. Take your time and do it right, which is exactly what any media consumer who cares about outcome wants.

9. Don't be a one-stop information shopper. Anyone wise enough to resist buying from high-pressure used-car salesmen also should be smart enough to read and watch and listen widely and not settle for getting the news totally from one source.

10. Evaluate the news you see and hear and read with at least as much attention as you put into buying a car. Don't tune it out with the excuse that it's all manipulative; if you do, you lose. Take news seriously. And when it is fed to you blended with entertainment —whether on "Murphy Brown" or "Hard Copy"—teach yourself how to figure which is fact and which is fiction. And if you think you're getting conned, say so. Demand the truth.

Patricia O'Brien is a veteran journalist and former presidential campaign press secretary. She is the author of the novels The Candidate's Wife *and* The Ladies' Lunch. *Her comments first ran in a longer essay titled "A Consumer's Guide to Media Truth," which appeared in the fall 1992 Media Studies Journal, "The Fairness Factor."*

15

The End of Predictability

James F. Hoge Jr.

For many in the American press, the collapse of communism and the Soviet Union ended what had become a predictable way of viewing the world. The Cold War was a simple measuring stick for determining the relevance and importance of international affairs. Events and trends were calibrated by how much they added to or subtracted from America's security versus its ideological superpower rival. This filtering mirrored the United States' clear foreign policy priority of containing communism's appeal and the Soviet Union's expansionism.

That measuring stick provided focus, but it also skewed the view. With the Cold War suddenly over, the U.S. public and its press shared a renewed awareness of the extent to which domestic problems had gone unattended while attention and resources were consumed in bipolar geopolitics. Equally startling was the fresh sense of those other international issues that had received lower profiles than their potential for damage warranted. Environmental degradation, population explosion, anti-Western animosities and economic dysfunctions moved from side events closer to center stage.

With the old gauges broken, the press is struggling to understand the new international order of risks and opportunities. The initial burst of euphoria when the Berlin Wall came down and democracy appeared poised to spread ineluctably across the globe was followed by dismay—sometimes despair—at finding the world unruly and unpredictable. The end of the Cold War may have resolved America's primary international problem, but not so for much of the world where, if anything, the cap has been released on an overheated radiator spewing up an array of old and new miseries.

At the same time, the news media's task has been made more difficult by an absence of clear, steady cues from Washington. Pretensions to the contrary, the press traditionally has covered international affairs from the perspective of America's perceived interests. This has meant explaining U.S. foreign policy and U.S. engagements, laced with criticism only when policy execution appeared to ill serve the nation's defined interests. Although most evident during the Cold War, this tendency has a lengthy lineage in American history.

Perhaps understandably, there is not yet an articulated official framework for U.S. foreign policy in a still-new post-Cold War world. Suffice it to say that the broad objectives so far espoused by the Clinton administration of promoting democracy and free markets are imprecise guides to America's interests, even less helpful to the media in formulating a post-Cold War agenda.

Deadlines don't wait on frameworks, and so the press has struggled to adjust on its own. Correspondents are finding the front lines of today's controversies—intellectually and physically—difficult to discern and often dangerous, indeed, in some cases fatal. Nor do the familiar centers of power, such as Moscow and Washington, carry the same assurance of being the right places for correspondents to congregate for the most important news of the day.

Reporters and their desk-bound editors also are learning that many problems are unfamiliar, involving as they do old ethnic rivalries, territorial disputes and historical wounds long ignored and thought to be dormant. In addition, the emerging agenda gives a higher, more constant priority to global management problems, such as the environment, requiring greater technical knowledge and more attention than they did when these subjects were subsumed under the bipolar rivalry. On both counts, educational updating is much in need through the individual efforts of correspondents and through academic refresher courses supported by media businesses.

Saddled with a more complicated agenda, the press must also perform for a less attentive audience. Released from the nuclear "terror factor" of the Cold War, traditionally insular Americans are even freer to concentrate on home and neighborhood. Except for the dramas of starving people and extreme violence brought into living rooms sporadically by television, the public is seizing the opportunity to turn inward. Fewer than half the Americans queried by pollsters this summer were familiar with the North American Free Trade Agreement. The lure of inwardness was never more apparent than in the last presidential contest, when voters elected a Vietnam War resister who promised to focus like a laser beam on domestic woes.

Thus, press coverage of foreign news finds itself squeezed off TV screens and out of newspaper columns by media executives worried about their bottom lines. Economic anxiety makes these decision-makers all the more prone to feed the public the easily digested fare of local news, lifestyle features and entertainment.

It is hardly new, but too much of today's coverage of international affairs focuses on the flash points of conflict rather than the evolution of trends. This characteristic is most pronounced in an era when TV dominates. Correspondents are "parachuted" into the latest strife, often with expectations that they will air knowing reports within a matter of hours. Film footage of violence is the element of foreign news most likely to leap the hurdles barring entry to the evening news shows' 22 precious minutes of airtime. For the many viewers for whom this is the main source of news, the picture of the world is limited, threatening and deeply distorted.

Regrettably, broadcast and print are both afflicted with diminished resources and reduced coverage of international affairs. The Associated Press, reacting to trends in the newspaper business, is ordering up from its correspondents shorter stories for smaller newsholes. The drought is most evident in local and regional newspapers. On a recent speaking tour through the Midwest, I stopped by the local papers. At one, a senior editor with little interest in foreign news said he published a modest amount of international fare, but still more than his taste would warrant. His reasoning rested not on a thesis of reader appetite, but rather on habit and past practice. At another newspaper, an editor with a strong interest in international affairs took the opposite tack. He read a number of dispatches and then performed the electronic version of spiking most of them because—unlike himself— he felt his readers weren't interested. Vague awareness of readership polls and management desires seemed to motivate his self-censorship.

Diminished attention to international events isn't strictly a phenomenon of regional and local papers. *New York Times* foreign editor Bernard Gwertzman told a Freedom Forum Media Studies Center interviewer in early 1993 that his space budget was down significantly in 1992. By then, the drama was out of the Cold War's demise.

In television, the cutbacks are more dramatic. The three main broadcast networks virtually have opted out of regular, noncrisis coverage of international affairs, drastically reducing their corps of full-time foreign correspondents and cameramen. CBS no longer assigns a full-time reporter to the State Department. Overseas, television relies increasingly on free-lance video footage and stringers, some of whose connections are suspect.

On air, the evening news shows are weighted toward domestic and lifestyle concerns and human-interest features. Moreover, the momentum is away from the evening news reports to magazine shows. *Time* magazine recently reported that such programs are now on air every night, consuming 10 hours of prime time every week, most modeled on the "60 Minutes" formula: three segments and a light closing feature. Content consists of consumer rip-offs, miscarriages of justice, exposures of sleazy characters—all presented in easily grasped, good-guy, bad-guy morality plays. Little of serious international affairs can compete.

By getting the airtime, magazine shows are where the "talent" wants to go. NBC's respected anchorman, Tom Brokaw, told *Time* that "it's getting harder and harder to find people coming into the business who want to cover daily news." This paucity can be understood as part of a larger problem—attracting the best young people into the news business in the first place. Contractions in both print and broadcast have meant fewer opportunities. Hiring and salaries are flat or down. Career mobility is limited. And foreign reporting suffers from a triple whammy. There is less of it, done by fewer people who must skip from place to place and story to story, often under dangerous conditions. There are some offsetting developments: Public broadcasting and CNN offer consistent public affairs coverage. Except for crises, however, these outlets claim only niche audiences.

While both broadcast and print are marked by reduced attention to international affairs, the disparity in those reductions is leaving the major newspapers as the only general-interest conveyors of regular, thoughtful dispatches on the world. A handful of first-tier newspapers maintain extensive networks of overseas bureaus and staff them with trained correspondents, many of whom have been taught foreign languages. Second-tier newspapers, also a handful, maintain some bureaus, fund consistent travel and make ample use of wire and supplementary service reports from overseas.

Foreign policy-makers speak as if they are bedeviled by the nature of post-Cold War press coverage, often alleging that it is television film footage that dominates agenda setting. They claim their hand is forced by pictures of human beings in distress accompanied by voiceover commentaries of the need for "somebody to do something," wryly noting that they now must explain why not to get involved in crises rather than the opposite.

For such critics, American intervention in Somalia was an example of television's power and its random selectivity in determining policy. President George Bush, so the argument goes, had to rid the screen of the awful pictures of starvation during his re-election bid, although he wasn't moved to exhibit a similar concern for the untelevised human miseries in conflict-torn Sudan or East Timor. And why, it is asked, is there clamor to "do something" about the savagery in the former Yugoslavia and not in the equally wrenching civil wars of Tajikistan, Armenia and Georgia? The former is close to the heart of Europe, but another distinguishing characteristic is that the Balkan conflict is a focus of Western media attention and the others are not.

While policy practitioners have a point, they press it out of proportion to reality. For example, the tragic pictures of suffering Bosnians have moved American viewers but have not in themselves congealed a strong consensus supporting U.S. intervention. The public is capable of a more complex assessment of its interests. In short, print and especially television can have a strong effect on policy-making, but not a dominant one unless there is a strong public will to act or unless forcefully presented government policy is altogether absent.

Many policy-makers see journalists devising their own foreign policy for the post-Cold War world, one that raises humanitarianism above vital national interests as a basis for actions and interventions. To non-Western eyes, this smacks of liberal imperialism and is to be feared more than Westerners understand. A sophisticated Asian diplomat, Kishore Mahbubani, writes in the latest issue of *Foreign Affairs:* "Most Western policy-makers today, who are children of this era, cannot conceive of the possibility that their words and deeds could lead to evil, not good. This is a genuine blindness. The Western media aggravate it. Most Western journalists travel overseas with Western assumptions. They cannot understand how the West could be seen as anything but benign."

Some of the pressure that squeezes out foreign coverage can be lessened by successful efforts to make the subject clearly relevant to readers and viewers. It is a legitimate expectation of news consumers, most of whom are taxpayers, to be shown the domestic tie-ins of policies pursued abroad. The press can do some of the tying on its own and even more as a conduit for officials, experts and businesspersons who know how to relate trade and aid to domestic economic health and dollars spent now to billions saved later. There is no more important subject for journalists to master in the post-Cold War world than the recounting of economic happenings and options and consequences.

Extra efforts to make international affairs interesting to a lay audience also can soften the gatekeepers who determine what goes on television and in news columns. Relating news through the experiences of human beings is especially compelling, and some of the best foreign coverage for general audiences consistently respects this premise. Making connections is another lure because it explains the implications of related subjects like population growth, environmental decline and the status of women. And increasingly, the nation's diversity can be used to capture interest in coverage of different parts of the globe.

Of course, not all news of importance can be localized, humanized or approached from a societal angle. Trade negotiations come to mind. Even here, a due regard for news consumers' concerns can transform what otherwise appears to be a distant abstraction. NAFTA is a current example. Both the press and advocates of NAFTA are emphasizing international reasons for the treaty, such as supporting Mexican political reform and strengthening relations with Latin America. More candid attention needs to be given to deep domestic worries about job loss, immigration flow and preservation of English as the nation's language. The latter might sound like an odd element in a discussion of trade negotiations, yet NAFTA promoters say it is one of the most frequently asked questions out on the hustings.

Policy-makers, however nonplussed by press performance, must recognize that the media comprise the modern forum. They must sell their policies through print, television and new communications opportunities being opened by advancing technology. An array of formats is available—the traditional press conference, town hall meetings, televised seminars like the one on economics in Little Rock, and long-form interviews with and without open phone lines. Bill Clinton's expertise in modern communications has been ineffectively deployed since coming off the campaign trail and into the White House. This is particularly true concerning foreign policy, where the president and his key associates have done little to explain their views of the nation's interests and the framework for policies to pursue them.

A final word should be said about the public's own responsibility to require and use the news it needs to make intelligent judgments on foreign policy. The point is self-evidently important: In a democracy, the public ultimately accounts for the nation's foreign policy and, in the case of the United States, the public's judgments carry the extra weight of determining how a superpower acts in the world.

The press is vital but not alone in the process of disseminating the relevant information. Linking citizenry and government is also the task of officials, scholars and nongovernment organizations with special stakes and concerns. As a key forum, the press can benefit from some rethinking both from within and from without. But it is clear, as Walter Lippmann observed years ago, that other institutions of organized information are necessary.

All of it, however, depends on reception. In 1955, before there was much television, *New York Times* publisher Arthur Hays Sulzberger made the point in terms of print, and it holds in today's broadened communications environment. "Along with responsible newspapers we must have responsible readers," he told a meeting of Southern publishers. "No matter how conscientiously the publisher and his associates perform their work, they can do only half the job. Readers must do the rest. The fountain serves no useful purpose if the horse refuses to drink."

James F. Hoge Jr. is editor of Foreign Affairs. *This chapter originally appeared in the fall 1993* Media Studies Journal, *"Global News After the Cold War."*

16

Follow That Tank!

Bernard Kalb

"Follow that tank!" It was more than just a kind of macho battle cry of war correspondents. It was also a kind of metaphor that caught up the spirit of journalistic roaming, of spontaneity, the chance to follow whatever story caught the eye, to explore different countries and cultures and people and try to make them come alive for readers and viewers back home. In those days, the desk in New York was on the receiving end.

Now it's the reverse, and I remember where the change began: in Saigon, from the mid-'60s on, with technological innovations that, like executioners, one after the other did away with distance and time.

First came the leased telex line from CBS News New York directly into the CBS Saigon Bureau in Room 206 at the Caravelle, clicking away at us. Suddenly Big Brother was watching. Then over the next decade came the satellite linking New York to the story wherever it was, reducing global mileages to seconds. Then came videotape, replacing film and speeding up editing. Then the portable instant voice link to New York. Then the portable satellite TV uplink. Even correspondents became portable, with the result that overseas news bureaus were closed down as economically and journalistically superfluous. The cellular phone was the final nail. There was no escape. By then, New York had synchronized all this gadgetry into an art form. *Live! Live! Live! Tiananmen Square! Berlin Wall! The botched coup in Moscow! All live!*

Now New York is everywhere, with the power to dial, call, summon, dispatch, edit. You're in the middle of nowhere and New York has still got you locked into its electronic cross hairs, trapped, triangulated, at the end of its global yo-yo string. They're barking in your ear: "Where's the script?" Off it flies into the ether via your computer link. They review it. Hurry, the "bird" is up, ready to go! So a crisis anywhere in the world is only seconds away, and so are you, flown into the midst of the story for moments before being ordered off to the next story. True, spot news and backgrounders still come in, but there's an ache for more time to flesh out your piece, more details, more context. But it's "bird" time, and off goes the piece, you're on the air, sometimes so fast, much to your own surprise.

The communications revolution was inevitable, the world at the touch of a button, and I'm really not complaining. But the *instancy* of today's journalism confronts us with a question: Has all the speed made for better reporting?

Bernard Kalb, former State Department spokesman and host of CNN's "Reliable Sources," began his career as foreign correspondent in 1955. His comments are excerpted from "In the Days of Carrier-Pigeon Journalism," which appeared in the fall 1993 Media Studies Journal, *"Global News After the Cold War."*

17

The Flickering Images That May Drive Presidents

Robert MacNeil

When the United States stumbled into Somalia, George Kennan, the revered scholar-diplomat, was appalled. It was a "dreadful error of American policy," he wrote, caused primarily by an emotional reaction to "the exposure of the Somalia situation by the American media—above all, television."

Kennan wrote to the *New York Times:* "[I]f American policy from here on out...is to be controlled by popular American impulses, and particularly ones provoked by the commercial television industry, then there is no place—not only for myself—but what we have traditionally regarded as the responsible deliberative organs of our government, in both executive and legislative branches."

Others weighed in—Secretary of State Warren Christopher: "Television is a wonderful phenomenon and sometimes even an instrument of freedom. But television images cannot be the North Star of American foreign policy."

Kennan concurred: "Fleeting, disjointed, visual glimpses of reality flickering on and off the screen, here today and gone tomorrow, are not the 'information' on which sound judgments on complicated international problems are to be formed."

Kennan and Christopher seem to suggest that television is usurping the function of responsible people in government to set the agenda in international relations and to define the national interest.

The point is carried further, yet somewhat differently, by Michael O'Neill, former editor of the New York *Daily News*. In his book *The Roar of the Crowd*, he says, "Thanks to the communications revolution and the new technology, the old world of diplomacy is in ruins."

The game used to be played by professionals, who considered public opinion a vulgarity and had only disdain for journalists and, more often than not, the statesmen who employed them. "Now, however," O'Neill writes, "every Tom, Dick and Harry is trampling over their red carpets. They are no longer the chief custodians of policy. Their arts are the arts of an era that disappeared...and ambassadors have become an endangered species."

Irritated by something George Shultz said on CNN, Jordan's King Hussein did not call his foreign minister or ambassador in Washington. He called CNN to broadcast his reply. Later, criticized for favoring Iraq in the Gulf war, the king again chose CNN as the quickest and most forceful way to get to President Bush.

In the Moscow coup of 1991, loyalists used a private national computer network with Western connections, as well as fax machines and portable radio transmitters, to mobilize support for Yeltsin. When the KGB shut down newspapers and radio stations, Yeltsin backers taped 10–minute newscasts and slipped them to the BBC and Radio Liberty, to be played in the West and back into Russia. O'Neill quotes Eduard Shevardnadze as saying afterward, "Praise information technology! Praise be CNN."

So television has enhanced communication between governments, but there is also TV's direct effect on presidents.

When President Reagan saw television pictures of the massacre of Palestinians in Lebanese refugee camps, he quickly sent in the Marines, an ill-considered mission that ended in tragedy.

Initially hesitant in the Moscow coup of 1991, President Bush decided whom to support only after seeing a defiant Boris Yeltsin on top of a tank—on television.

After the Persian Gulf war, Bush was determined not to be drawn into Iraq's internal battles, confident that the blows he had dealt Saddam Hussein would prompt his overthrow. Instead, Saddam attacked the Kurds and pictures of their misery were so affecting that Bush felt forced to intervene to protect them.

Do these examples mean that television is driving presidential foreign policy? Let us hope not. What television has done is to bring public opinion into play as never before in determining where national interest lies and what policy will further it.

It may be a mighty inconvenience for policy-makers. Public ventilation usually is, because the public is a bull among the delicate porcelains of the experts, indifferent to the endless nuances of those trained to see them. But I would agree that it is also, at bottom, more democratic.

It should not surprise us that television, which has modified all our institutions, should be altering the conduct of public and international affairs.

In medieval Europe, the church was a matrix of thought, the boundary of popular imagination: It explained everything. Today, television sets the boundaries of the popular imagination, and it sets them wide, if rarely very deep.

There has never been a phenomenon like television in its ubiquity, its seductive appeal, the passive absorption it encourages, its lifelikeness, its companionship, its ability to leap across international frontiers and over the barriers of class and literacy. What hyperbole can you possibly imagine of a medium that has African tribesmen who live close to the Stone Age and Queen Elizabeth in Buckingham Palace both doting on the same television program—"Dallas"?

The only thing that people on average do more than watch television is work and sleep. And if they don't have work and can't sleep, they watch television. Though it may be eroding literacy, it sells millions of books. Though academics deplore it, they, too, seek the social legitimacy that television exposure confers. And so on.

Television has created a different order of public opinion. In the issues that touch foreign affairs, the public witnesses the same apparent reality as its leaders. The public is no longer a mass to be sold a policy after it is decided. It is now active in seeing policy made and, one might even say, getting policy made. Witnessing the same images, of course, is the political opposition—loyal or not—able to use them like any other evidence to challenge the competence of government.

Television is the public window of the information revolution and its noisiest voice, capriciously alighting here, departing there, dramatizing this issue, ignoring that one, governed by the need to be fresh and attract an audience. It seeks out controversy, violence and all the heartaches of the world with an insatiable appetite for novelty. Those with an idea to sell, a cause to push and outrage to call to the world's attention seek out television.

In Somalia, it was not merely the pictures that wrung the hearts of the public: The pictures were made more eloquent by the words of Audrey Hepburn of UNICEF and Mary Robinson of Northern Ireland. Chief among those who seek out television are governments and politicians, because it has become indispensable. For political leaders in modern democracies to complain of television is like Angelo in *Measure for Measure* condemning fornication while he plots it himself. Governments are not virgins in television; they are in bed with it.

Secretary of State Christopher says television images should not be the North Star of foreign policy. But television images are quite acceptable to the White House when they made the Gulf war look like a giant video game and sent Bush's approval ratings into the 90 percent range. Television images are quite acceptable in getting presidents elected, that is, in choosing the leaders who will make the foreign policy. Fleeting, disjointed, visual glimpses of reality—in Kennan's phrase—now dominate the central right of our democracies.

Ever since politicians discovered how to adapt public opinion sampling and consumer mass marketing, image making has been how they won office. But it does not end there. Even once in office, governments cannot chuck the image-making habit, and, increasingly, government policy is marketed by images—the making of foreign policy becomes in part a contest of images: Televised images condition the public. Constant opinion polling measures their highly simplified views. Politicians react to the polls.

But governments are not passive victims of television. When Margaret Thatcher, Ronald Reagan and George Bush each wanted to go to war without the inconvenience of hostile public opinion, they let television see only what they wished it to see in, respectively, the Falklands, Grenada, Panama and the Persian Gulf. No more Vietnams for them. Governments live by television—and they may die by it—but to deplore its influence is disingenuous.

Television inherited its definition of news from print journalism, evolving as a merchant of news who better understood how to harness curiosity for profit. Television journalism came of age in the Cold War and, for decades, the Cold War framed the worldview. But suddenly, like governments, scholars and foreign officers, the media were cast adrift from these secure moorings and needed a new way of looking at the world. Television in particular has found it in humanitarianism, an observation I credit to a briefing paper on foreign policy and the press prepared at the Media Studies Center last year.

The arrival of marvelous new technology, especially lighter cameras and portable satellite uplinks, makes it possible to broadcast instantly from anywhere. There has also been sudden access to many regions previously closed by the Cold War. And in the Cold War's wake has come a surge of nationalist and tribal violence, providing an unlimited supply of suffering humanity. Television deals best with people, not ideas. The human consequences of the Cold War were often hidden from view. But now, violations of human rights from many causes are manifest to the cameras.

Also emerging from the Cold War has been a United Nations eager to fulfill ambitions long frustrated by a divided Security Council, to intervene and keep peace and alleviate suffering. Yet the instinct to intervene clashed with other realities: a global recession that sapped revenues, increased unemployment and aggravated the painful industrial restructuring caused by the same electronic revolution that drives the new information order. These realities produced a countertrend—the urgent political need to repair and convert economies distorted by the Cold War.

Confronted by a heady mixture of all these trends—a proliferation of peacekeeping and peacemaking initiatives running into budget and social deficits, and a rising clamor from new isolationists —governments were battered simultaneously by calls to do something, do everything, do nothing. In this confused period, the Kennans and Christophers see television whipping up the public to drive government into action.

While that was the initial wave in Somalia and perhaps in Bosnia, another wave followed in reaction. As television watched the United Nations mission in Somalia appear to founder in violence, as the casualties—particularly American—mounted, the political barometer swung quickly toward withdrawal, forcing President Clinton to articulate his goals more precisely and to set a time limit on the U.S. presence.

In Bosnia, ghastly images of suffering provoked not a clarion call for decisive intervention but, for two years now, a creeping sense of impotence and resignation, as the complexities and moral relativities grew more apparent to the public and government alike.

As Roger Rosenblatt, editor in chief of *Columbia Journalism Review*, noted recently in a commentary:

> Too much may be made of the power of pictures. They often give a quick rush, like a dose of sugar, but the rush also wears off quickly, leaving the mind with facts to sort out. And people seem to understand that this is true. Otherwise all anyone would ever need to get us into a war would be a TV camera, and that has not been the case. It has not even been the case in Somalia. Every picture is one side of an event, often the outside. Sometimes we want to see it, only it. Sometimes we want to see through it.

American presidents used the rush of sugar for different purposes. George Kennan said Bush probably assumed the public would be as enthusiastic about Somalia as about the Gulf war, permitting him to leave office "with a certain halo of glory." In Bosnia, it suited Bill Clinton's purposes as a candidate to chide Bush for inaction and to promise stronger measures if elected. Those measures—air strikes on Serbian gunners and arms for the Bosnians—proved to have no international support, so he settled on relative inaction. Then the mortar bomb fell in a Sarajevo market, appalling the world and galvanizing it to action, particularly the Europeans who had opposed Clinton's call for air strikes. Narrowly—very narrowly, despite the universal outrage—NATO voted its ultimatum to the Bosnian Serbs to pull their guns away or have them bombed. In this case, television created a consensus President Clinton had been unable to create by his own energy or moral authority.

To say that either Bush or Clinton was the prisoner of a popular cry for action generated by television pictures is to ignore political calculation, their wish to harness the occasion for political as well as humanitarian purposes. By and large, both the media and the public tend to follow strong leadership, capable of identifying the clear national interest in a course of action. It remains true in the television age as in the past: The foreign policy agenda is driven by the president until, instead of riding the tiger on a particular issue, he lets it ride him. While he is in the saddle, television acts as his megaphone, explaining, selling, critiquing his policy and acting as a catalyst in the chemical reaction between opponents and proponents of a polecat within government and outside.

If television senses that the country generally approves of a policy—especially with troops in the field—it amplifies particular action to the point of stupefaction. But when events slip into the saddle and ride the leader, then television will loudspeak his helplessness, inaction, seeming impotence or overreaction. Think of Jimmy Carter in the Iran hostage crisis.

By focusing attention and raising the temperature, modern media and the polls they generate increase the pressure on a political leader, not necessarily to act impulsively but to be decisive. So the alarm sounded by Kennan seems to mean this: Political leaders must not be in thrall to the powerful new media.

But in democracies today, no modern leaders take office unaware of that media power in shaping public opinion. They used it themselves to win office, and they have to continue to use it to hold office. Instantaneous television coverage from around the globe has made the media impact on popular opinion more dramatic. It has put a greater premium on a government's ability to react quickly and to make clear statements about the national interest.

If officials like Warren Christopher do not want television images to be the North Star of foreign policy, they had better point to the star they *are* steering by. Or as President Clinton recently put it, rather inelegantly, they need to find the "bumper sticker."

The information order forces governments and presidents to enter the lists of public argument more quickly and more forcefully than might have been necessary in more languid times. The flood of information delivered by the new media encourages public opinion to doubt that elected representatives or public officials have a monopoly on wisdom, or any inspired perception of the national interest.

In this climate, policy achieved in open dialogue with an aroused and attentive public, although more difficult for policy-makers, must be a better policy than one concocted behind closed doors and communicated as through divine revelation.

So, some conclusions: Television and instant global communications undoubtedly make the conduct of foreign policy both more difficult and, at times, easier. The technology reduces the option of governments to ignore events or to take its time in responding to them.

There is now instant global witness to man's inhumanity to man, in a manner that converts hitherto abstract situations into palpable cruelties that engage our feelings and test American idealism—and its pragmatism—as never before. Such images may reinforce a government's intentions, creating a mood for intervention abroad, or may run counter to them, creating an instant mood for withdrawal.

Television raises the price of not intervening because evidence of suffering assaults our sensibilities. But it also raises the political price of intervention by so graphically illustrating the cost.

In doing all this, television's attention is capricious, fitful, easily distracted by other stories, driven by traditional imperatives of journalistic competition to be first, most graphic, not to miss what others have. Television today seems driven by self-promotion, a desire to draw attention as much to itself as to the event being covered. This is not a new value, but in print this motive used to be blatant only in the tabloid press. The effect is magnified because the new technology increases the size of the media pack every year. Any tiny station hungry for a bit of credibility (or driven by genuine journalistic curiosity) can now send a camera anywhere and get sensational pictures. As the pack grows, so does the impact on the country. When one person on a small ship shouts, "Look over there!" everyone stampedes to look and the ship lists or perhaps capsizes.

The cumulative effect increases the pressure on a president and his supporters in Congress to be certain of their course and clearly in command. It increases pressure on a president to define the nation's interest and to communicate that definition constantly, a far easier task in the bipolar world now vanished with the Cold War. If the president can define that interest clearly, television—however lurid, responsible or irresponsible—will not drive foreign policy. When he fails to do so, it may.

Robert MacNeil is former executive editor of the PBS "MacNeil/Lehrer NewsHour" and an author of nonfiction works and novels. This chapter originally appeared in the spring 1994 Media Studies Journal, *"The Presidency in the New Media Age."*

III

What Kind of Future?

18

Peering Over the Edge

Ken Auletta

Since 1985 the networks have been staggered by an earthquake that struck as if in slow motion, cracking their foundations. By the end of the 1990–91 season, the damage was unmistakable. In a single season they had lost 5 percent of their viewers, as the three-network share of audience fell to 62 percent. Since 1976 the three networks had lost one out of three viewers. Cumulative profits of $800 million for the networks shrank to $400 million by 1988; they will probably lose money in 1991. By 1990 a relatively new competitor—cable—boasted revenues of $17.8 billion, dwarfing the $9 billion of the three networks.

On top of this, a recession began to pound the networks in 1990, and profits sank. At the end of the year the CBS network would lose about $30 million. While the ABC network earned about $225 million in 1990, by the fourth quarter its profits had begun to tumble. At NBC, Bob Wright did not meet his $465 million profit goal for 1990, as after-tax earnings fell to $340 million, half of which came from the network. Privately, Larry Tisch confessed early in 1991 that he feared CBS's network losses could climb above $200 million for the year and perhaps as high as $300 million. Dan Burke, the longtime chief operating officer at Cap Cities who had succeeded Tom Murphy as CEO, said it was "easily possible" that the ABC network would lose money in 1991. Early in the year, Wright alerted Jack Welch that NBC would miss its overall profit target for 1991 and that the network itself might lose money.

Falling revenues and rising costs invoked new economies at the networks. In December 1990, Tisch ordered yet another round of cuts, this one totaling $70 million; he also brought in McKinsey & Company to help him streamline and take a closer look at how to spend money more intelligently. By February, long before McKinsey's report was ready, a gloomy Tisch was impatiently pressing for $200 million in cost savings, including $100 million immediately. Period. End of discussion. Dan Burke, like Tisch, said ABC would seek to alter functions and better analyze its spending; he, too, foresaw nothing but trouble ahead for the networks. Unlike Tisch or Wright, he said he would struggle to avoid layoffs, though he wouldn't make an ironclad pledge. Unlike Tisch, he would follow a deliberate process and not just issue commands. Wright early in 1991 asked each NBC division to devise a cost-saving restructuring plan, including massive layoffs.

What explains the sudden collapse of network revenues? The causes are many. The recession obviously gutted advertising budgets; as network audiences shrank, advertisers sought other outlets; the decision of the networks to try and make up for lost revenues by running from 4 percent (ABC) to 8 percent (NBC and CBS) more ads altered the psychology of the marketplace, shifting leverage to advertisers who had no reason to panic since they now knew network time wasn't scarce. The war with Iraq took a toll as well. In its first days, the war cost each network up to $6 million a day in lost advertising; NBC calculated that the Gulf war cost it $50 million between Aug. 2, 1990, when Iraq invaded Kuwait, and February 1991, when a cease-fire was achieved.

In a less quantifiable way, the war in the Gulf may have cost even more. Instantly the public glimpsed the cataclysmic changes in the television industry. Viewers realized that CNN, not the three networks, was the channel of choice for live, up-to-the-minute news. With relatively few overseas bureaus, the networks no longer qualified as a worldwide news service, if they ever had. Even though the war boosted interest in news, by early 1991 the three network newscasts together attracted only 54 percent of those watching television, a loss of nearly one out of three viewers in less than a decade. All at once, everyone seemed to be talking about whether network news had a future—indeed, whether the networks had a future.

Rewind to 1986. It's clear, in retrospect, that in many ways the new owners succeeded in changing the old culture. They tamed the unions, forced News and other divisions to spend less, convinced everyone that the good times had stopped. Doing business with cable was no longer heresy. Nor was the idea of producing and selling programs to a network rival, as ABC announced it was prepared to do. Nor was the idea that the four News networks should pool their efforts on Election Day exit polls, saving about $10 million each in the process. The new owners had forced their organizations to recognize new competitors. How could they not? It was now commonplace for the media to identify Fox and CNN as "networks"; programs that had once been "free"—the movies, the Olympics, boxing matches, football games, perhaps one day the Super Bowl or World Series—viewers now paid to watch.

The new owners helped awaken the networks to the encroaching earthquake. In this, they were right.

But in their quest to find fresh sources of revenue, they rushed to eliminate barriers that actually protected their investment. Overlooked was the fact that some barriers were meant to protect, say, News from entertainment values or from advertiser pressure, or to protect consumers or children from hidden advertising. At NBC's annual management retreat in 1990, for example, many of the 160 executives questioned why Sales or Entertainment couldn't have more input into news specials, or why News tended to keep its distance from the rest of the company, as if it were somehow special. The panic for profits had provoked Bob Wright to suggest that maybe Don Johnson of "Miami Vice" could host some news documentaries, and Jack Welch once to propose that publishers pay to induce the "Today" show to interview their authors. In their haste to impose a new order, to defend shareholder rights, sometimes the new owners failed to see the unintended damage to their investment and to their public trust.

In many other ways, the new owners had changed and become more like the old ones. Larry Tisch and Tom Murphy set out to curb Hollywood costs under their control, slashing the budgets for their self-produced series and made-for-TV movies. But within a few years, they were copying NBC's 1986 decision to produce more of its own shows. "We should have done it sooner," admitted ABC's Murphy.

"We didn't because we went through a learning process. There were too many other things on the table." The new owners began by focusing on costs and ended thinking more about revenues. No one any longer had to sell them on the magnetic power of hit shows, or the importance of spending time in Hollywood.

The new owners were zigging and zagging more, no longer assuming that a straight line was the quickest way to reach their goals. Sometimes the new owners felt compelled to make decisions they knew might be counterproductive. For instance, in 1990 NBC agreed to pay the producers of "The Cosby Show" a nearly $3 million weekly license fee, or about $75 million annually; this expenditure cut in half NBC's $100 million profit from its entire Thursday night schedule. The new owners were determined to reduce sports-rights fees and stars' salaries, yet both rose. They might want to change it, but the habit among the three networks was like the rule of thumb in the arms race: If one superpower acquired a weapon, the other wanted it. So they became bigger spenders, as Larry Tisch did when he paid $3.6 billion to broadcast sports or $50 million to acquire 10 movies from Universal. Despite the caution in spending money, Murphy and Burke would approve multiyear contracts for Steven Bochco, James L. Brooks and other Hollywood talent, as well as Diane Sawyer.

Why were the new owners, three shrewd, cautious investors, sometimes so extravagant? One reason is that they learned the value of investing in hits. Since they didn't control their producers, they had to pay what the Hollywood market demanded. Their affiliates also demanded attractive products, particularly sports. And in the network business, like any other, you keep customers happy.

Another reason is that their peer pressure group changed. "When the new owners come in, no matter who they are, they come into an established system," observed Creative Artists Agency's Bill Haber. "When David Puttnam came in and tried to change the motion picture business, he failed." What happened to the new network owners, said Haber, is what happens to isolated cells in the human body: "The amoebic reaction breaks down their cells, not the other way around. Think of it as a giant corpuscle. The outside body absorbs the new cell."

But this is not the complete answer. Still another factor was how human logic—ego, vanity, anger, pride, even panic—sometimes triumphed over business logic. The networks were a strange new world for these conventional businessmen. Good news wasn't just measured in stock prices and profits. They became so eager to hush critics, calm affiliates, send a reassuring message to Hollywood and Washington that they occasionally overspent. Sometimes it was simply the desire for victory that proved irresistible. "In no other business do you get a report card every day from overnight ratings," said a ranking ABC executive. "Over a period of time your competitive ego gets determined to fight hard for these things." To win.

The desire to win is more pronounced in a business that imposes unusual constraints on the power of the chief executive. The new owners thought they would be hailed for cost cutting, yet were vilified instead. Surely it was no fun for Larry Tisch to come home to his Fifth Avenue apartment and see Local One stagehands handing out leaflets telling neighbors, "Next time you see Larry Tisch in the elevator or the lobby, tell him you are outraged with his efforts to destroy the lives of his employees." Nor was it much fun for Tisch to admit, as he did early in 1991, that "we overpaid" for sports. Nor was it fun for these businessmen to spot what they believed to be waste, and yet do nothing for fear that cuts would ignite a public furor. Larry Tisch, who believed when he first acquired stock in CBS that it was "just like every other business," would eventually conclude that he had been "much too glib." The mysteries of programming, the difficulties of dealing with 200–plus affiliates, of appeasing government regulators and fulfilling a public trust while under a public microscope, said Tisch, "set network television apart and complicated the normal logic of business planning and budgeting." Even Jack Welch, who believed that networks were different from other businesses only in the attention the media lavished on them, acknowledged that daily press coverage—including a story that very day that NBC had curbed its distribution of photocopied press clippings—had an effect on an organization and its leaders, sending spirits up or down, producing energy or lethargy.

Fast forward to the future. The network owners knew that they would encounter increasingly negative publicity, more audience erosion, more cost cutting, as they struggled to shrink their organizations. In the future, sports will probably continue to migrate to cable and pay channels, since these can better afford to subsidize the salaries of Roger Clemens and Dwight Gooden. Maybe some or all of the networks will program fewer hours each day. To save money, maybe game shows or even syndicated programs will be stripped into prime-time hours. It is no longer unthinkable that one of the Big Three might abandon the network business altogether.

Unless network news consolidates more of its functions with other networks or local stations or overseas news services, as each is vying to do, it is likely to see its influence ebb. It's possible that one or more networks will abandon news, merge its overseas operations, or eliminate a nightly newscast and instead sell news packages to stations. Increasingly, news is viewed as an important but expensive luxury. The three networks together spent about $1 billion on news in 1991, compared to about $200 million by CNN. News "isn't the strategic center of what happens here," declared Jack Welch in early 1991. While Welch praised Michael Gartner, Tom Brokaw and NBC News for their work, he nevertheless noted, pointedly, "Fox doesn't have news." Because news was now available on local stations, CNN, PBS and elsewhere, in the view of Welch and no doubt others, "News is not the core of the asset." This was his financial calculus.

Journalists have a different calculus, which is why the clash between shareholder responsibility and the public trust will not subside. As he sat one night in a Miami bar reflecting on NBC's 1990 management retreat and how executives who attended seemed to have "bought into" the GE lingo and value system, Gerry Solomon was morose. He had been at NBC News for 17 years, and he was now the executive producer of "Sunday Today" and "Meet the Press," but when his contract expired in 1991 he said he probably wanted out. Here's why: "The argument we hear all the time is that 'quality' counts. But the definition of 'quality' has changed at the networks. They are not talking about the quality of the reporter"—they would just as soon send a green local reporter to cover unrest in Nicaragua as they would the experienced Garrick Utley. "They are talking about the 'quality' of the payoff to the network." He meant that Welch and Wright were talking about costs. Yet journalists talked about "ephemeral things" like "credibility" and "calling" and the "quality" of the product. "GE doesn't know these things because they can't be quantified," he said.

If news or sports or other network functions become expendable, will the three networks themselves die?

Probably not. Certainly there are powerful forces with a stake in strong networks, starting with advertisers. Ten years ago, said Roy J. Bostock, president of D'Arcy Masius Benton & Bowles, the world's ninth-largest ad agency, 60 percent of a company's marketing budget was earmarked for advertising and only 40 percent went into promotion. Today, he said, only 20 percent goes to advertising. "That's a major part of the problem that the networks have." It's also a problem for the advertising business, "because how goes the television business is how goes the advertising business." With advertising growth stalled, agencies often saw their fate linked to the networks. Hollywood studio chiefs, as Disney Chairman Michael Eisner and Warner Chairman Bob Daly acknowledged, also had an interest in robust networks. The networks were their biggest single customer; no one else could match the license fees paid by the networks, or their mass audiences; no one else could create an audience for shows that can be sold to syndication, which is where the studios make big money.

The public also has a stake in the networks. Whatever its failings, a mass medium creates a sense of community. Americans grow up believing diversity is good and bigness is bad, which is often true. But it is also true that the public has an interest in a common communications system, in the larger public purpose a network can perform when it brings a disparate population together to share an experience. Often this potential is unrealized. But it was fulfilled when the networks became the nation's common church after John F. Kennedy or Martin Luther King Jr. were assassinated; or when nearly three-quarters of all viewers tuned to the miniseries "Roots"; or when the new owners sacrificed ad revenues to offer live coverage during the first week of the 1991 war with Iraq. Ev Dennis, executive director of The Freedom Forum Media Studies Center at Columbia University, observed: "We have shared values that are enhanced by three networks. For the same reason, we don't favor 500 languages in the country. It does create a national consensus of values and of what we think is important. We could be like Italy, where the newspapers are weak," TV is dispersed, and there is no national consensus. The stability of the American government and society, he said, owed something to the networks.

It is also true, however, that the variety of choices now available to the TV viewer enhances the diversity of the culture. For nearly two decades the federal government has sought to deregulate television in order to encourage a greater range of choices; yet at the same time government has long proclaimed the public's right to free television. The two goals sometimes war. As is often true in a democracy, individual freedom may not mean equal access. Freedom of choice may belong only to those who can afford to pay for the opportunity. If there were no networks, how many citizens could afford—or have access to—cable or pay TV? How could 50 cable and pay-TV channels, none with more than 2 percent of the audience, subsidize quality programs at prices all consumers could afford? Will the public tolerate limiting major events to cable when only 60 to 70 percent of the nation has access to it? While he has a personal interest in building this case, Larry Tisch correctly identifies the public policy question looming down the road: "The issue is the future of free television. Will citizens have to pay $50 to see the Super Bowl? Or $10 to see a made-for-TV movie? That question will be there. And when the crisis comes, it will be too late." Ten years from now, he predicted, Congress may wake up and call for an investigation into who killed free TV.

Because powerful interests—the public, the government, advertisers, local stations and the studios—have a stake in network television, it is entirely possible that government will one day pass legislation to protect "free" TV. It might suspend the fin-syn rules, allowing the studios and the networks to merge, thus enhancing the economic viability of the networks.

What *is* certain about the future is this: The networks can never recapture their monopoly. No matter what advertisers or the studios or the government say, having tasted the power to choose, viewers will continue to insist on programming for themselves, just as they increasingly opt for the convenience of shopping at home through catalogs. It may be unclear how the networks will tap other sources of revenue, or with whom they will ally themselves. It may be unclear what technologies will emerge—high-definition TV, direct broadcast satellites, fiber optics, digitalized signals, among countless others. What is clear is that the programmer will be king.

A decade ago, Michael Eisner, then a top Paramount executive, told of a visit he made to the Consumer Electronics Show in Las Vegas. There he wandered among the exhibits for videocassettes and videodiscs, giant screens and miniature television sets, 100–channel cable systems and backyard dishes, car phones and home computers. "Everywhere the call of technology. The music of progress was in the wind," he remembered. Eisner panicked when he realized that his studio, Paramount, was not even on the main exhibition floor. "Somehow, we had missed not only the show, but the boat." Were the studios not part of the brave new world of tomorrow? Then as Eisner walked past the exhibits of the latest technologies, he noticed that each was playing movies starring Warren Beatty, John Travolta or some other American star. None promoted "Fukkatsu No Hi from Japan."

The future, Eisner realized, belonged to "the product," the entertainment shows and movies produced mostly by Hollywood. Everything else—the VCR, the cable wire, the local stations, the satellite dish, even the networks—was merely a way of distributing his product.

What seems certain is that if the networks are to thrive and perhaps survive, they must be permitted to produce and own more of the product. The networks need to find a way out of their trap, which is that they rely on a single source of revenue and are but three channels in a 150–channel universe. Standing alone, the networks may die. With additional revenue sources or partners, the good times may return.

Ken Auletta is a columnist for the New Yorker *and author of* Three Blind Mice: How the TV Networks Lost Their Way. *This chapter originally appeared in a longer form in the fall 1991* Media Studies Journal, *"Media at the Millennium."*

19

Media Complexes and Juvenile Distractions

Vitaly Korotich

It seems to me that many people in the United States have still not gotten used to the fact that life there has become sufficiently stabilized, that cowboys no longer spur on their horses as they hurry West. Even American cooking is still oriented to the horseman: It's a fried piece of meat, a baked potato, a glass of cold water—and then you must be ready to gallop on.

The same applies to American newspapers. In large part, the American press is for people who don't have time to read. One of the youngest and most aggressive newspapers in the country, *USA Today*, is clear evidence of this, with its short articles and a bare minimum of material requiring thought. Intellectuals get their daily nourishment from the *Los Angeles Times*, the *Washington Post*, the *Wall Street Journal*, the *New York Times* and a few other newspapers on the East Coast. But even in those newspapers many good pieces are lost in an ocean of advertising, like computer disks stored haphazardly among pop music CDs.

Outside the United States, these same American newspapers are the

sources for the *International Herald Tribune*, one of the most respected dailies from Paris to Singapore. In it everything is put together
seriously, with the greatest respect for the foreign reader. It is the
American national newspaper of Europe. But there is no comparable
paper in America; television has become the national newspaper by
default. I would like to think that this is not a remnant of the days
when American artists and writers had to go to Europe in order to
become famous. The label "Made in the USA" has long possessed a
high reputation all over the world, but many American media are
burdened by complexes and juvenile distractions that are really not
indicative of American life. Be that as it may, the correlation between
the different types of mass media does not give birth to information
empires on the order of the Soviet model, where all information—in
newspapers, on radio, on television—was until recently directed from
a single office.

America is one of the models for cooperation among different
peoples, and its media provide much of the energy for change elsewhere in the world. The impact of CNN, for example, is tremendous.
No matter where you are, in any respectable hotel in the world (even
in Moscow), it is now possible to receive the latest news from Atlanta
24 hours a day. CNN and the *International Herald Tribune*, perhaps
without realizing it, have become the prototypes for tomorrow's mass
media, uniting us in humanity. America's mass media, I believe, will
inevitably give birth to a type of publication that will interest many
people. It only remains for Americans to understand that today they
are not so very different from other people, including the Europeans,
who are now undergoing a process of unification into their own United
States.

Vitaly Korotich, former editor in chief of the Moscow newsweekly Ogonyok, *is a
professor in the College of Communications at Boston University and a columnist for
Radio Liberty. His comments are excerpted from "Songbirds of the System," which
appeared in the fall 1990* Media Studies Journal, *"World Media."*

20

Media Globalism in the Age
of Consumer Sovereignty

Anthony Smith

The long West European search throughout the 1980s for a cultural counterpart to the continent's movement in politics culminated in 1989 in the publication of an important European Community Green Paper, *Television Without Frontiers.* Its purpose was to allow the national programming of Community members to circulate throughout the Community—in short, "a common market for broadcasters and audiences." The plan was clearly designed to help shift European television towards commercialism and away from its traditional public service nature. Accordingly, a crucial tenet was the effort "to secure the free flow of information, ideas, opinions and cultural activities within the Community."

Yet the Green Paper also called for the creation of a trade barrier to limit American entertainment imports—in the name of national cultural "preservation." To the powerful lobbyists in the Motion Picture Association of America, the Community's talk of quotas was simply a blow at their legitimate commercial interests. To the Europeans, the MPAA appeared just to want to grab a vast new market that might cover for Hollywood's uncontrollable cost spiral while simultaneously turning Europe's 350 million people into cultural vassals of America.

The ensuing debate has been long and fierce, the outcome still uncertain as I write. There is a widely shared European fear that transnationalism in all its forms, even when it issues from the EC offices in Brussels, is inimical to the whole tradition of nationally based broadcasting to national audiences. But the opposition is not primarily nationalist in character; rather, it springs from the same source as the widespread private and public fear of globalization.

In many countries today—including some in Central Europe — information media are passing into the hands of nonresidents. The (originally) Australian Rupert Murdoch, for example, now enjoys un-challenged ownership of newspapers in Britain, the United States and elsewhere, not to mention the burgeoning transnational satellite station Sky Television. Whole sections of the entertainment industry, tradi-tionally part of national, city, local, regional, or ethnic political and social life and manners, are passing into the control of managements whose outlook is exclusively global. Is this just a facet of the ending of the nationalist phase in world history? Is the ownership of large enterprises irrelevant to a company's ability to respond to the cultural needs of specific audiences? Indeed, is the oft-expressed anxiety about media internationalization based on a nostalgic, sentimentalized and patronizing view of popular culture?

Such an anxiety is rooted in the belief that the world is losing the logic of indigenousness and therefore a kind of authenticity; that, where our hope was that the media would act as means of reconciliation, they are turning into instruments of homogenization; and that technology will, in the forms it has actually taken, deprive us of a home under the pretense of giving us a larger one.

Globalization—the concentration of a substantial number of the world's information and entertainment businesses into a series of huge international companies—has been under way for over a century. This is especially true of national news agencies (wire services) and maga-zine firms, which even in the 19th century were starting to shrink into a tiny group, dominated by French, German, British and American firms that divided the world according to the spheres of influence of their respective governments. The anxiety this provoked was a straight-forwardly political one: To what extent would those governments influence the shaping of news values or even deliberately manipulate the information that circulated around the globe?

The problem today, just as irreversible, is also more intractable. The worldwide extension of three familiar processes—chain owner-ship of newspapers, cross-ownership between media, and acquisition of media by ordinary industrial concerns—means that national gov-ernments cannot easily enforce even the modest rules some have adopted to regulate or impede these processes (though even free enter-prise governments on the whole do not like major newspapers passing into foreign hands: Australia recently foiled Robert Maxwell's attempt to purchase a paper there).

The paradox of the present phase of corporate change is that it is occurring at precisely the moment in technological history when it has become extremely cheap and, in practical terms, easier than it has been for several decades for new firms in all media to enter the mar-ket. It costs little to start a radio station, and much less than it did in the 1960s to start a local television station; publishing has been trans-formed by the arrival of desktop computer equipment; book stores have multiplied throughout the developed world, making it much easier for authors to find their readers. Digitization is similarly transforming video production and recording; through cable it is becoming annually easier, in theory, to acquire whole television channels for specialist services, and it is relatively cheap to reach audiences within a given city or region. Deregulation, espoused by politicians in country after country, should be guaranteeing this great opening of the information and entertainment market. It is the age of consumer sovereignty.

The end of the 20th century ought to be witnessing a transformation of the media industries into hundreds and hundreds of small compa-nies. That anyway is what was predicted at the start of the computer revolution. This was supposed to be the end of "mass" society.

At present we can see—often in the same societies at the same time—a process of Hollywood-style cultural homogenization on the one hand, and on the other a paradoxical determination by govern-ments to encourage new competitive enterprises. To some extent the proliferation is indeed taking place. While the new giants are gobbling up the smaller giants everywhere from Buenos Aires and Hollywood to Paris and Tokyo, armies of small-scale entrepreneurs are also estab-lishing themselves. In France, the talk is of Hersant, Maxwell,

Berlusconi—but also of Teletel, of scores of new radio stations, of a new cohort of artisanal filmmakers. But everywhere the talk is of their vulnerability, of rationalization and takeover, of small independents taking over tiny ones or all of them having to take shelter together in the bosom of a Behemoth. In Britain the 400–odd small production companies conjured into existence by Channel Four in the 1980s still, a decade later, have only a tiny number of potential buyers. The new cable and satellite channels are in practice commissioning very little work, the BBC has barely started to honor its commitment to buy from the independent sector, and Channel Four itself will soon be competing for the sale of its own advertising time and may be drawn into the competition for large audiences and cheap production.

The process of globalization also opens up the issue of ethnic and political pluralism. The new ubiquity, via satellite and cable, of television channels originating in America, Britain and perhaps France can only be at the expense of the smaller nations and ethnic groups within them. Of course, the promise always embedded in the new technology was that entrepreneurs within minority audiences would find ways of making commercial channels work within the compass of a small ethnic or national community, but beyond a few vaunted experiments this has yet to occur. Politics, not markets, seems to be the only effective savior of minority cultures.

One cannot adduce audience figures in support of such a contention—rather the reverse. The marketplace gives expression, almost unanswerably, to the needs of consumers. But perhaps as citizens we hold preferences that our behavior as consumers does not reveal. The simple fact that we cheerfully used to buy ozone-unfriendly hair sprays does not mean that we were freely deciding that we wanted a polluted atmosphere—merely that the consumer choices available were not organized to help us articulate the more collectively beneficial choice.

It has always been the task of the press and broadcasting to act as conduits for the flow of information and debate. Democratic societies could not really exist in the absence of such a facility. But the Western media consist of enterprises that function within a market economy, and markets are prone to concentrations of control and the amalgamation of competing forces for mutual protection. The new climate provides enormous advantages and opportunities for companies that combine previous rival information businesses. Even media institutions that operate from the public sector of market-oriented societies are caught up in the vortex of fresh corporate temptations.

But democracies tend to feel that citizens should be exposed—in reality as well as in high-minded theory—to a multiplicity of sources. Ongoing amalgamation throws this essential pluralism into jeopardy; while it can be argued that the sheer dynamic of the open market compensates by creating new pluralistic openings, it is increasingly possible for people to fail in practice to be exposed to competing views and outlooks. In the new culture of diversity a person has to choose his or her sources of competing intellectual influence rather than to chance upon them willy-nilly.

Today, in the era of privatization and the worldwide scramble for the acquisition and control of media industries, we need to understand more clearly how the industrial giants who control vast areas of the information and entertainment media affect the evolution of national and world cultures. And, even more urgently, we have to inquire whether individual societies should seek to limit or channel the process of global amalgamations in the interest of maintaining fundamental freedoms.

The method by which newspapers are manufactured and distributed, for example, has always had profound implications for what might be called the moral condition of journalism. Newspapers, like all the other newer media, have always had to balance not only their commercial and intellectual roles, but also the overlapping and sometimes conflicting needs of readers and advertisers, proprietors and editors, sources and governments. Press freedom, however essential, has never been absolutely available; at any moment it depends, obviously, upon prevailing constitutional and legal arrangements, and the attitude of the current government—but also on the way that the medium as an enterprise is being managed.

Governments (and other institutions) have always seen the media as potentially rival sources of authority. They have concerned themselves with the nature of the cultural forms (pamphlets, books, Bibles, newspapers, the novel) that emerged from the press and from the other technologies of information and entertainment.

The regulatory systems that were developed to govern modern communication devices derive ultimately from the bureaucracy for licensing and registration that grew up to cope with the newspaper. In electronic systems for delivering information we are witnessing a kind of ultimate extension of periodicity, for in electronic mode the information source is permanently present; we have learned since the arrival of radio and television what had already been suspected in the late 19th century—that information media shape the realities of a society, interact with the processes of government and provide the terms of the relationship between governors and governed, even (perhaps especially) in totalitarian societies.

Regulatory systems evolved to police, select, control or otherwise demarcate the boundaries between media; to prevent concentrations of what was deemed to be excessive power; to calculate the consequences of media operations in order to counteract them; to make certain that those in control of specific media command the trust of government; to guarantee forms of economic competition sufficient to prevent the evolution of monopolies. It is this regulatory paraphernalia that has largely drawn the map of the media world today. In the United States, for example, the doctrine of localness governing the franchising of broadcast outlets and the legal limits of the number of local stations in a network, added to the controls on cross-ownership of media and other doctrines governing monopoly, fairness and business practices, have between them created the American broadcasting system as we know it. In turn, the changing of the regulatory systems now taking place in many countries is today bringing about a reworking of all the boundaries on the world's media map.

Each technological transformation has occasioned its own appropriate organizational devices, what one might call its "enterprise formation." The characteristic form of the newspaper of the 18th century was a printing house that took in jobbing work and added books and periodical publications as a way of using its capacity to the full; that, in turn, was determined by the working practices of a highly organized work force divided into minute craft specialties. The newspaper of the 19th century required far more working capital to operate, with its growing teams of correspondents attached to the new technologies of the telegraph, and began progressively to detach itself from the general printing business. It became more technology specific. Newspaper owners remained close to the world of political patronage, their independence being secure only when their readership was sufficient to cover their increasing costs.

The 20th-century newspaper has required still larger quantities of capital—but it has found itself through its dependence on advertising deeply implicated in the general market economy. The newspaper since World War I has ceased to be dependent on the economics of the political world, earning its income from its citizen readers, and has become more wholeheartedly an instrument of advertising. The newspaper and the magazine (and broadcasting, too, in some societies) quickly became engines of the 20th-century consumer economy, their information fueling the growth of tastes and fashions, their internal economics greatly influenced by the cycles of trade. Writing in 1922, Walter Lippmann said: "The real problem is that the readers of a newspaper, unaccustomed to paying the cost of news gathering, can be capitalized only by turning them into circulation that can be sold to manufacturers and merchants. And those whom it is most important to capitalize are those who have the most money to spend." Lippmann was noticing, as many others were at the time, the nature of the new tension with which the newspaper editor had to live.

Since the 1920s we have seen the growth of group ownership of newspapers, and the reduction of competition among daily newspapers within given markets. Since the early years of the century there have been repeated dire prophecies of the loss of an essential disinterestedness in journalism as a result of the growth of newspaper combines, and many fitful attempts to stop newspaper proprietors from gobbling one another up. But the process has seemed relentless except where governments have provided financial subsidy and/or vigorous regulation.

The new economic system establishing itself in the media industries throughout the world entails an emphasis on the ownership of information itself rather than just of the mechanically produced forms that information takes. Narrative fiction, for example, plays a part in publishing, in magazines, in cinema and television, and the same work can find a place in all of these media in a world market. Publishers want to be in a position to exploit a work of talent across the whole media landscape; they have come to fear the consequences of being excluded from an audience if they do not have a finger in every kind of media pie. Furthermore, it is becoming easier in technological terms to become involved in a wider range of media. Transnational media empires are thus coming into being to exploit new opportunities and as a protection against possible losses of opportunity. Newspapers, film businesses, radio, television and publishing are passing into the same institutional hands.

In many countries such linkages have long been thought to be a danger to society, and in some cases the law has sought to prevent them. But to turn back the present tide altogether would be to stand in the path of the inevitable—and the commercially necessary. Audiences appear to want the new diversity of information that is the counterpart of the new concentrations in media ownership. A viewer can choose to see a film on video, on cable or satellite or (later) on conventional television, or can read the book instead, possibly published by the same company. The new enabling technologies are arriving as a result of other wider changes in telephony, in electronics, in the exploitation of space. National legal systems are helpless to prevent the arrival of alien television channels from unregulated satellites, and in any case markets are no longer containable inside the inherited national forms. It is impossible to regulate the media and information industries in one way and the markets for apples in another.

Right across the industries of information, whether based on text or image, whether based on paper or cathode-ray tube, these unfamiliar contemporary economics now prevail, and politicians and regulators see it as their duty to help, through deregulatory measures, to force margins down and thus serve the consumer. Together with computerization, deregulation is one of the engines of globalization.

The result is that all of the companies concerned are driven towards self-protective merger, scale economy, constant self-reorganization and a search for the ultimate in rationalized markets. Few really quarrel with the legal, institutional and political motivations behind this activity; however, no one has calculated its moral consequences. It is possible that some will conclude that there aren't any, that information goods are fundamentally the same as others and that we all benefit from the results, whatever they may be, of the enforced efficiencies of deregulation and a more competitive economy.

But this change is also producing consequences that tend to conflict with other socially desirable objectives, among these the maintenance of diverse sources of ownership in the companies that produce our information and entertainment.

So great are the institutional and corporate changes that are flowing from these fundamental shifts in technology and in the prevailing conceptions of communication that it is difficult as yet to discern all of the implications for society. It is hard to see where the fundamental requirements of a society actually lie. We are used to a pattern of newspapers that work in mutual competition and in competition with radio and television. We are used to cinema and television living in a state of mutual tension, and in joint competition with video. We think of newspapers and book publishing as completely different businesses. In particular we have been brought up to see the newspaper as a lightly or entirely unregulated medium and television as highly regulated, with obligations of impartiality imposed because of its powerful political presence, its highly persuasive nature.

However, we are moving into an era in which the distinction between the corporations that own these different entities is impossible to draw. The processes of the new technologies and the pressures generated in the new regulatory environment are suggesting to managers of these enterprises that survival and further growth depend upon mergers and alliances across the political divides. That which nations are powerless to prevent does not of course automatically become desirable, but it does become necessary to ask again what the former prohibitions were intended to protect or secure and to see whether society can achieve the same objective by some easier means.

There has been little research into what one might call the intellectual consequences of media monopoly. In a modern society with its many sources of potential influence upon opinion, does a decline in competition between newspapers, say, really matter? In 1989 the London-based Broadcasting Research Unit carried out a comparative opinion survey of the readers of the three News International-owned British national daily newspapers, the *Times*, the *Sun* and *Today*, with those of other journals. The three papers concerned have all consistently taken a broadly similar editorial line on a number of public issues affecting the future of the media, and thus of great moment to News International itself. All of these papers have supported the abolition of the license fee on which the BBC has traditionally been funded; they have celebrated in banner headlines the launching of the first satellite channels available in Britain; and they have argued that the BBC should be obliged to take advertising. (The continued existence of an adequately funded BBC could mean that a large portion of the

British audience at any moment would be watching something other than Rupert Murdoch's Sky TV.)

The BRU found that readers of the papers concerned are markedly more likely to be "critical of terrestrial television; to welcome new channels; and to oppose the license fee"—a profile that is not consistent with these papers' readers' political leanings, nor with their demographic profile. The editor of one of the papers agreed that its intention was "to destabilize the set-up" of British television. Should a media enterprise use the influence of one of its parts (and that inflated by multiple-title ownership) to pursue the interests of another? The readers, it may be argued, know what they are reading and ought to be able to discount arguments—perfectly legitimately advanced—that they suspect of being tendentious. But can they? Do they? The argument that they may choose no longer pertains in the era of the information of abundance, for a democratic society requires that contradictory opinions should actually reach a large proportion of people, not merely that these opinions are somewhere available. That is the heart of the problem. In the old and familiar media environment, dominated to a great extent by the public sector bodies, the problem was concealed, or perhaps just ignored. We are living through the aftermath of mass society; the new media environment is one in which it is decreasingly likely that entire populations will be subject to the same shared flows of information and participate in the same pool of common allusion. Yet behind the diversities are new homogeneities in information and entertainment—a circumstance allied to the emergence of the new media empires and the new generation of media moguls.

Take, for example, the recent wave of transactions that have taken place within the international film industry. In practice there are seven film libraries and film studios that fill the needs of the world cinema market. They are all based in the United States and have been accumulating their stores of movies for up to 70 years.

In the 1980s these studios have discovered that more and more sales income is available outside the United States as a result of the arrival in country after country of the electronic and consumer revolution. VCRs are everywhere. Acquiring a film library is like discovering an overlooked seam in an unused gold mine. But the U.S. domestic market remains the most profitable in the world.

There are, however, five or six countries in the world where there are entrepreneurs who wish now to enter the U.S. film market, and to do so they realize that the easiest route—perhaps the only one—is to acquire one of the existing seven "majors." That is really the constituting principle of globalization—the desire to enter an established media market that is wholly clogged by indigenous occupants, one of which is available for merger or acquisition. That is why companies located thousands of miles apart have suddenly discovered the potential benefits of globalizing, even in cultural industries that have been traditionally bound to a national, local or ethnic remit. The worldwide growth in the demand for entertainment materials has outstripped old constraints and inhibitions. The prospects for future growth are so great as to fuel a constant pressure towards acquisition and consolidation.

In 1988 the U.S. majors earned $1.13 billion in domestic sales. Foreign earnings alone in 1990, however, are likely to equal domestic revenues, even though the latter are still increasing. Those figures help to explain why in 1985 Rupert Murdoch's News Corporation was keen to acquire 20th Century Fox for $575 million and why the Qintex Group of Australia paid even more a few years later for United Artists. Meanwhile the relatively small but then rapidly growing British company, TV South, decided to buy MTM entertainment—a deal that later turned sour. Giancarlo Parretti of Italy bought a controlling interest in the Cannon Group, having already acquired France's Pathé Cinema. The objective of all of these transactions was to expand into a business that was undergoing a rapid upward leap in its overall operations around the world but of which the U.S. market remains the bedrock.

The moving image has not been the only targeted medium, of course. Hachette of France acquired the Grolier Company in 1987, as well as the Diamandis magazine group; Hachette paid $1.2 billion in all, and thereby established a business with an annual sales figure of $4 billion, half of it outside France.

It was the linking of Time and Warner that produced the largest single media enterprise hitherto known anywhere in the world; the merged company had a total sales figure of $8.7 billion. In some ways the merger could be seen, at least from the point of view of Time, which had had an unhappy experience with cable in the 1970s, more as an old-style defensive merger than a new-industry "synergy." At the moment the Time-Warner merger was announced, stock markets rumored bids for Time from Germany's Bertelsmann and Rupert Murdoch's News Corporation. Time was a farraginous mixture of businesses, containing among them book publishing and some cable (including the successful HBO). Warner had added the Lorimar company to its already successful film and television interests, but this, too, was more to ward off predators than out of a deliberate corporate plan.

The Time-Warner marriage set off a wave of fears for the survival of pluralism in the American media. Rupert Murdoch already owned *TV Guide*. Time already owned Little Brown. So would print media, owned by a moving-image entrepreneur, still feel free to criticize the latter's product? Was there to be a collapse of proper journalistic standards? Would television news programs transmitted by one of these companies criticize the movies (and books) produced in the same group or deliberately castigate or ignore those produced by a rival group?

Familiar critics of the U.S. news media such as Ben Bagdikian and Joshua Meyrowitz, Todd Gitlin and Nicholas Johnson, have all warned that such consequences are inevitable. "The lords of the global village have their own political agenda," writes Bagdikian. "Together, they exert a homogenizing power over ideas, culture and commerce that affects populations larger than any in history. Neither Caesar, nor Hitler, Franklin Roosevelt nor any Pope, has commanded as much power to shape the information on which so many people depend to make decisions on everything from whom to vote for to what to eat." The dangers are of course precisely those expressed, but as yet there is little evidence that they are real. Indeed, a whole new world of independent companies has emerged in many countries, and these remain outside the newly homogenizing forces, the new global empires of information.

We are now living in a society in which the information industries have become basic to the economy rather than peripheral, and it is almost accepted that some restriction on multimedia ownership and on excessive information power generally are justified. The public interest, always hard to define, must lie in the provision of a diversity of information sources and therefore in limiting the concentration of ownership. Otherwise the democratic process itself is placed in thrall to a company or individual that may be pursuing, albeit quite legitimately, ends that are at variance with other objectives of society. But it cannot be assumed that every example of transnational ownership is an infringement of a society's rights. Far from it. While a danger may well exist, it must be more important to maintain ease of entry for a new voice than just to keep an unviable newspaper or station out of the hands of someone who wants to buy it.

If the majority of our information and entertainment passes into the control of half a dozen companies (which means in effect half a dozen individuals), then this would indeed constitute a danger, whatever the policies and attitudes of the corporate managers themselves. In such circumstances, government itself would come to be conducted at the behest of this self-selected group, and this would even raise the question of whether direct control by national governments would not be more "pluralist."

But we are far from that. The first requirement of the present day is a clear and disinterested monitoring process, a collecting of global information about the growth of global companies within the media (including entertainment) industries; this will help us to chart the course and see whether it is in practice tending towards the feared quintopoly. It is not enough to watch the growth of giant corporations; it is equally important to see whether small media companies continue to spring up and develop from other nonmedia companies. Are newspaper titles continuing to grow in number? Are the new radio and television outlets passing into the same hands or into the hands of newer companies? Are the latter surviving?

The second requirement is for a flow of real case history from every part of the world. It is one thing to measure freedom of expression through oppression. We know from the specialist human rights organizations how many journalists and writers and filmmakers around the world are actually in prison, and what fresh repressive legislation has been passed. But that does not tell us really about the moral condition of the media in what one might call normal circumstances.

One great difficulty about this new phase of media research and media mapping is that it requires those very societies that have been used to doing the observing to scrutinize themselves critically. Researchers tend to be concentrated in certain countries of the developed world and are not on the whole geared to asking these kinds of questions of their own societies.

Their task is made more difficult by the fact that the questions that need asking are without obvious answers. There are only 15 towns in America with competing daily papers—out of 1,500—but the shrinking of the American press into a series of city monopolies has not in itself crippled the flow of information in America; on the other hand, has it deprived a vast number of Americans of access to really crusading journalism within their communities? To take another example, does Sony's control of a Hollywood major necessarily mean that one section of America's movies will be any less humane in approach or less numerous or less relevant to American society?

What we need to understand are all of the cultural implications of the rapidly changing media map of the world. We obviously bring old questions to the table, but we may well emerge with new questions, with new fears probably replacing old ones.

Anthony Smith is president of Magdalen College, Oxford University, and former director of the British Film Institute. This chapter originally appeared in the fall 1990 Media Studies Journal, *"World Media."*

21

The Inevitable Global Conversation

Walter B. Wriston

Many years ago, a noted historian delivered a speech titled "How to Achieve the Inevitable." In this particular instance he was talking about the peace that would follow World War II, as it was clear that the war could not go on forever; yet, even as portents of allied victory grew stronger, there was a growing doubt that we could translate victory into peace.

I was reminded of this in reviewing some of the papers that have been delivered at this Center about how to achieve a national policy on information services. Some would argue that policy is already in place and spelled out in the Bill of Rights in our Constitution. Americans have always wished for an open society. John Adams in his *Dissertation on the Canon and Feudal Law* put it this way: "Liberty cannot be preserved without a general knowledge among the people, who have a general right . . . to that most dreaded and envied kind of knowledge. I mean of the characters and conduct of their rulers."

The first great advances in information distribution had little to do with government, and everything to do with private enterprise. I refer to the idea of a public library open to all. The first libraries in this country were started by ambitious groups of young men like those assembled by Benjamin Franklin, who eventually founded the Library Company in 1731. Franklin was but the first of many public-spirited citizens engaged in this pursuit. There were also many private collections like the one John Harvard gave to a small college in Boston and the combinations of private collections that John Bigelow helped assemble that became the New York Public Library. The eleemosynary tradition continued and more than 2,700 free public libraries were established by Andrew Carnegie, some with matching public funds, in towns across America. To a certain extent their growth and utility were made possible by what we would now call software written by Melvil Dewey in 1876 that permitted the efficient cataloguing of books.

Of course, not everyone has ready access to a library, and some are still unaware of how to use one. The Library of Congress, for example, permits anyone over high school age to use its huge collection, but the harsh truth is that what the elite regards as great books are often left on the shelves and the "trashy" romantic novels have a waiting list. The elite has always believed that it knew what was good for us and could make choices for us. The concept reached its apogee in the writings and subsequent action of an Italian journalist named Mussolini: "Fascism," he said, "denies that the majority by the simple fact that it is a majority can direct human society. . . ." Traveling through Italy at that time one saw huge posters bearing Mussolini's picture and the caption "He will decide." Mussolini is long gone, but the urge to decide for others survives.

The good news is that the Information Age is making this kind of mind control impossible because there are just too many pathways for news and data to find their way to us. Some worry about this. Media scholar Leo Bogart, for example, complains that "an information highway that's jammed with the likes of Jimmy Swaggart, Madonna and Ice-T can easily be a road to nowhere," and that "knowledge is not distinguished from fact, lies from truth, the real from the imaginary." Just who is to make these judgments is left unsaid. He might have been describing a modern bookstore featuring a book on the conspiracy theory of President Kennedy's assassination, or how the American mind has closed, or even Madonna's contribution to our culture. This attitude in its extreme form can result in Nazi-esque book burnings or, closer to home, in the quaint New England practice known as "Banned in Boston" or in what is now called "political correctness" on some college campuses. Sometimes it is the government that picks out what is good for your mental health.

Media mogul Rupert Murdoch put it this way: "While a lot of British TV is of high quality," he said, "I don't know how many of you want to watch 350 to 400 hours of snooker . . . or 60 to 70 hours of darts," but, he said, "I doubt you'd like being compelled to pay a $110 annual license fee on your television to finance BBC." Fortunately, Mr. Murdoch has given the British many channels to choose from, and they are exercising that right in increasing numbers. Often what they choose to watch does not sit well with the BBC establishment, which complains about the invasion of American TV programs that, in its view, have little redeeming value. In the meantime, the British TV police prowl around in their vans stuffed with electronic gear, looking for a TV viewer who is watching without having paid the license fee.

We need a whole new look at the regulatory framework built by Judge Harold H. Greene, the Federal Communications Commission, the public utility commissions, congressional committees, the various cable laws and tax-code depreciation schedules. Technology is moving much faster than the processes of government. While bureaucracies hunt for old distinctions that technology has erased, alert political leaders use the technology for their own purposes. In the midst of one of the recurring crises in the Middle East, when Jordan's King Hussein wished to reply to some statement made by then-U.S. Secretary of State George P. Shultz, he did not summon an ambassador to launch a formal protest but rather booked himself on CNN. At the same time that the president appears on "Larry King Live," other branches of his government regulate many phases of our society as if we still lived in the Industrial Age. Fortunately for us all, the market has a way of supplying what people need or want if the government gets out of the way, or sometimes even if it doesn't.

The original reason advanced for the regulation of the airwaves by the government was that it was believed that only a limited number of broadcasters could use the air at one time. There was, we were told, a spectrum shortage, so the public interest would be served by regulating the airways in such a way as to assure access to all. Apparently, the government believed that there was no shortage of newspapers, so they would not be subject to the so-called Fairness Doctrine (now happily retired but not dead in the hearts of Congress). Technology soon made obsolete the premise on which the regulation was built. We now use the spectrum at frequencies deemed impossible just a few years ago; doubtless this is just the beginning. In addition, the advent of cable, fiber optics and satellites has overwhelmed the regulators. Information technology is moving data and information, in author Michael O'Neill's words, "across the barriers of space, illiteracy, and national sovereignty to reach virtually all of the inhabited earth. . . . Equally significant, much of the information is being delivered in an oral-visual form that breaks the monopoly of the world's literate classes."

This has permitted what I call a global conversation. The implications of a global conversation are about the same as that of a village conversation, which is to say, enormous. In a village there is a rough-and-ready sorting out of ideas, customs and practices over time. A village will quickly share news of any advantageous innovation, and if anyone gets a raise or a favorable adjustment of his or her rights, everyone similarly situated will soon be asking for the same. And why not? These people are just like you and me; I see them and hear them every day. Why, the villagers ask, should *I* not have these things? And so the virus of freedom travels on the global network. And no matter what governments do, the word will get through.

All of this creates huge problems for established power structures. In the past, the educated elites could read about democracy or capitalist prosperity. But hearing or reading of such things is not at all like having them happen in your village, happen to people you can see and hear, people just a few streets or broadcast frequencies away. A global village will have global customs. In a global village, to deny people human rights or democratic freedoms is not to deny them an abstraction they have never experienced but to deny the established customs of the village. It hardly matters that only a minority of the world's people enjoy such freedoms or the prosperity that goes with them: Once people are convinced that these things are possible in the village, an enormous burden of proof falls on those who would deny them.

Even though television reaches hundreds of millions of people on our planet, and although the law of technology is the law of convergence, each sector of the industry here at home has dug in to protect its turf. It is only human nature for people to resist changes that threaten their pockets or their beliefs. Those who know what we should see and hear for our own good will fight a rearguard action to "protect" us from ourselves. We have, for example, the complaint of Tom Lewis writing in a recent issue of this *Journal,* lamenting the success of the Rush Limbaugh show. "Is our 'Doctor of Democracy' really serving us?" he inquires. "Does his success signal a triumph for our free expression? Is this glut of hot air really our victory in electronic democracy, or should we, like Pyrrhus, say, 'Another victory like that and we're done for'?" In calling the program a glut of hot air, Lewis passes judgment. But one person's hot air is another's wisdom. Is this not the age-old cry in modern electronic dress of people complaining that the world is in danger because my particular viewpoint is not demonstrating the same ability to get accepted in the marketplace of ideas as the views of my enemy?

Some 150 years ago, one of the keenest observers of the American scene, Alexis de Tocqueville, observed: "The nearer men are to a common level of uniformity, the less they are inclined to believe blindly in any man or any class. But they are readier to trust the mass, and public opinion becomes more and more mistress of the world."

I would argue that all of this is good news for freedom. Democracy is an act of faith, but it is also based on individual responsibility, and the more information that can be supplied the better the judgments should be (although it does not always work out that way, as today's scientific truth may be tomorrow's joke). Sometimes passions of the moment subsume good judgment. But as the concept of freedom travels on the network at near the speed of light, and as more and more of the world's population know there is a better way to be governed, public opinion, in Tocqueville's words, becomes "mistress of the world." While people worry, sometimes with good reason, about the extremes of the right or the left, Washington talk show host Diane Rehm wrote recently, again in the *Media Studies Journal,* "Given a variety of opinions on any given subject, people will sort through what may be conflicting ideas and find a way to make sense of the most complicated issues."

In addition to the myriad TV images transmitted around the globe, new private computer networks proliferate. While experts debate the shape and structure of tomorrow's data networks, the number of computers connected to networks grows at an exponential rate, and almost everyone agrees that the future almost inevitably is one in which most of the world's multimedia terminals can be connected to each other. While some in government draw up grand multibillion-dollar plans for a superhighway of information, many different companies and universities are already building one—the principal impediment to building the information highway being the government itself. The Baby Bells, with their huge cash flows, are still laying hundreds of thousands of miles of copper wire at home, but abroad bid to install long-distance fiber-optic cable. Congress has awarded cable TV monopolies in every city and then passed laws designed to lower the rates to consumers, but has succeeded only in creating even higher tariffs. In the meantime, the struggle for Paramount Communications is making allies of book publishers, home-shopping networks and Baby Bells. This list goes on and on. The national planners, past and present, of the fading socialist age have never understood the answer to Carl von Menger's question: "How can it be that institutions that serve the common welfare and are extremely significant come into being without a common will directed towards establishing them?" Perhaps a modern-day economist might even be thinking of the thousands of bulletin boards on the network that, like Topsy, just grew.

In America, the well-founded fear of concentration of power helped structure the regulatory framework that was designed to prevent media monopoly. Technology has shattered that monopoly. In simpler days newspapers competed with each other and with radio and television. Newspapers were almost immune from government interference while TV and radio were heavily regulated. Today the distinction between all forms of purveyors of news and data is being erased by technology while, at the same time, information and intellectual capital have become the most important factors of production in our global economy. Knowledge, which at one time was a kind of ornament for the rich and powerful to display at conferences, is now combined with management skills to produce wealth. The vast increase in knowledge in the last decade has brought with it a huge increase in our ability to manipulate matter, increasing its value by the power of the mind and thus generating new substances and products unhinted in nature and undreamed of only a few years ago.

The world is changing not because computer operators have replaced clerk typists, but because the human struggle to survive and prosper now depends on a new source of wealth: information applied to work to create value. Information technology has created an entirely new economy, an information economy, as different from the industrial economy as the industrial was from the agricultural. And when the source of the wealth of nations changes, the politics of nations changes as well.

The transition from one form of wealth creation to another is usually at first denied by the establishment that sees its power eroded, and only reluctantly accepted when it is clear to all that a change has occurred. For thousands of years, people were nomads wandering from pasture to pasture. Land was not regarded as an asset, and wealth was counted by the number of cattle one owned. When village agriculture began to appear, land became a form of wealth. Rules were laid down about ownership and water rights, and power moved away from tribal chieftains toward territorial rulers. Later, with the advent of the industrial society, making things in a factory was perceived as creating wealth, but as usual the establishment fought it. Even so sound a person as Benjamin Franklin dismissed such a notion. "Agriculture is truly productive of new wealth," he said, but "manufacturers only change forms, and whatever value they give to the materials they work upon, they in the meantime consume an equal value in provisions."

Today, with the emergence of information as the pre-eminent form of capital, once again the establishment is threatened. This change affects not only the creation of wealth, but also military power, the political structure of the world and how business must be structured and run. Conquest and control of territory is rarely worth the cost these days. When natural resources were the dominant factor of production, control of land seemed a sure way to enhance sovereign power. Today, war tends to destroy or smother intellectual capital, which is totally mobile.

The pathways open to the transmission of data and information are now so prolix as to make national borders totally porous and old regulatory distinctions meaningless. Intellectual capital will go where it is wanted and stay where it is well treated. Any teen-age computer nerd knows this, but a federal bureaucracy spent around seven years trying to decide where computing stopped and telecommunications started. In the end it gave up.

As both the speed and bandwidth at which data are transmitted have increased to near the speed of light, the value of some information has an increasingly short shelf life. What might be called the time value of information now is reduced in some instances to a few seconds. In today's world, the value of a currency is determined by the price the market will pay for it in exchange for some other currency. Indeed the market is no longer a geographic location, it is tens of thousands of computers linked together worldwide. This network has created the Information Standard that has replaced the Gold Standard. Unlike all other previous international arrangements, governments cannot call a press conference and resign from the Information Standard—regardless of what they say, the screens will still light up and the giant vote-counting machine that is the global market will render judgments on the value of a currency. Central-bank intervention is doomed to expensive failure as the size and speed of the market overwhelms governments. Governments do not welcome the Information Standard any more than absolute monarchs embraced universal suffrage.

Information technology has forever changed the way the world works. It has changed the way wealth is created. It has changed the concept of sovereignty as borders become totally porous. Any such profound change causes disruption in the lives of nations and individuals. Instant communication does not in and of itself create understanding. Advanced technology does not produce wisdom. It does not change human nature nor make our problems go away. But with much trauma and dislocation, it does speed the world on its journey to more freedom for more people.

Walter B. Wriston, former chairman and CEO of Citicorp, delivered these remarks as part of the Media Studies Center's inaugural Technology Lecture Series address. This address originally appeared in the winter 1994 Media Studies Journal, *"The Race for Content."*

22

Highway to the Stars or Road to Nowhere?

Leo Bogart

"Information highway" is an unfortunate metaphor for the emerging telecommunications system. Like the Holy Roman Empire, which was neither holy nor Roman nor an empire, it will not be a highway, nor will it be dedicated to information. On a highway, traffic moves (at best) in only two directions, but communication saturates a multidimensional universe. The number of potential contact points is almost infinite, since they include all the people now alive and all those who have left their traces behind them from the past.

The phrase "information highway" comes from the vocabulary of technicians preoccupied with the mechanics rather than the substance of communication. Next to meaningful symbols that people can borrow and exchange, the tangible connections of copper or glass are inconsequential. Engineers reduce "information" to electrical charges that can be digitally translated into zeros and ones; in those terms, all images, sounds, musical tones, signs and ideas can be described as "data." In an electronic sense, *any* signal that can be communicated is "information," but everyday parlance distinguishes between messages that have some real or imagined utility and those that primarily serve to pass time.

If we look upon future communication systems simply as means of transmitting data, the principal questions that arise are those of sorting these data—combining, selecting, assigning priorities and setting limits on them. There should be no problem in generating input in a world in which all existing information becomes obsolete as quickly as it is produced and in which the main problem is one of avoiding overload rather than of having the well run dry.

These days, the pre-eminent use of telecommunications for *mass* communication (as distinct from *interpersonal* communication) is for entertainment, not for information. The soaring use of 1–800 and 1–900 telephone numbers provides a lesson: Nynex alone gets 11 million calls a month to the 1,000 "information services" it carries. Forty percent of them are for "adult" lines.

The use of the telephone makes all media interactive, but it requires live human operators at both ends of the wire. Two-way, broadband communication networks give interactivity a new dimension. They allow viewers to play games, respond to quizzes, order merchandise and services, manipulate camera angles at sportscasts, select among possible conclusions to dramas and mysteries, and find kindred souls with whom to exchange confidences and gossip. There is a market for interactive media, just as there is a market for traditional parlor games, but interactivity requires a measure of effort and energy that most people are unwilling to expend, since it is the demand for passive, easygoing entertainment that brings them before the tube in the first place. Cable and the VCR have boosted the dominance of Hollywood over the nation's leisure hours. We watch drama on film and television, read novels and comic strips, and listen to music on recordings or the radio because these activities divert us. They may leave some residue of instruction, but that is not their primary appeal.

Whether they inform or entertain, mass media are distinguished from individual communications by their packaging. An interactive video or multimedia computer program permits a high degree of personal selectivity, but it is not an individual communication because its elements must be prepared and formatted in advance, just like the contents of a newspaper or radio program. *Better Homes and Gardens* might produce a special edition for podiatrists who own aviaries, but it would still be a mass communication, not a personal one.

It is misguided to think of the 500 promised video channels as if they represented 500 presentations in real time rather than 500 files of different kinds. (Five hundred is a nice round number, taken out of the air; there are potentially an almost infinite number of channels from which to select.) In the short run, with more cable channels available than there is programming to fill them, many will inevitably be used to repeat the same offerings at different starting times. Simplified video recording and storage devices should eliminate the need for such redundancy.

The future home communication system will not be analogous to today's television set, but rather a device for summoning up the whole available pool of printed publications and audiovisual recordings. Speed-calling systems will allow users to go immediately to familiar and favorite sources, to browse or to cull selections from a larger database, much as library goers can quickly locate the books they want in a computerized catalog.

Telecommunications will stimulate totally new productions and will also open up huge stores of existing archival resources. After all, only a small fraction of what currently flows through existing video channels represents communication in real time—many (but not all) news, sports and public affairs programs, for example. Most entertainment, by far, is prerecorded, and there is no technical reason why it could not be retrieved directly by a home receiver.

Can we expect a continued increase in demand for new media content? The public turns to the mass media for novelty as well as for the reassurance of the familiar. Human beings have an endless craving for surprises, as long as the unpleasant ones do not hit too close to home. They accept innovation only within limits and look for novelty within those limits. No one would tolerate watching the same soap operas over and over again, or listening to only one tune; few would accept, as many of our ancestors did, the endless ritual rereading of only one book. That is why new works are constantly produced and why they find audiences.

Communication has been occupying a larger share of the nation's consumer economy, but this share cannot continue to grow indefinitely at its present pace. It is limited both by time and money. The day has only 24 hours, most of them occupied by sleep, meals, work, school, chores and other necessities that interfere with potential media exposure (although meals and chores have in good measure been absorbed into the broadcast day). This means that new media choices will take audiences and revenues mostly from each other and is why television audiences have remained at approximately the same size even as the number of choices has continued to grow.

But is there enough of a supply of talent to meet the demand as channels multiply? Creative endeavors activate the senses and emotions. Most of the time, in popular culture, this experience is trivial and transient. True innovation is scarce, virtuosity is precious and the pool of available human talent always seems pitifully small relative to the demand. If this has always been the case, the deficiencies are bound to be amplified as telecommunications expands the array of televised choices.

There is already much increased competition for the existing supply of content and for the people who produce it. (Consider the battles for control of Hollywood's film libraries.) This competition has already raised to outrageous levels the incomes of entertainers who are in short supply, like outstanding basketball players and film stars. But competition also makes the market for talent more volatile, since reputations are to a large degree the contrived creations of promotion, which is easily diverted to new rising stars.

Will programming come from abroad? National cultural boundaries can be crashed by winning confections of formula entertainment, as Hollywood's overseas revenues attest. Media enterprises are increasingly global in scope, and the search for talent will intrude more foreign films and television programs onto the American screen. But past experience, especially in the motion picture industry, indicates that they are unlikely to attract significant audiences. Americans are both linguistically and culturally ethnocentric; they find dubbed sound tracks and subtitled translations equally unacceptable. Thus, programming needs will be satisfied from domestic sources.

Expanding the number of media outlets is unlikely to increase the incidence of literary or artistic genius in the population. An infinitesimal proportion of the output is produced by the likes of Orson Welles or Federico Fellini, whose efforts are often commercially unsuccessful. Most media content is churned out to order by individuals with journeyman skills that might readily have been transferred to other occupations. Just as failed novelists and actors end up as car salesmen or primary school teachers, there is an endless supply of salesmen and teachers whose penchant for writing or acting might be put to work in media industries without noticeably altering the character of the output. The present quality of television programs, with dozens of cable networks competing for directors, writers and actors, is not noticeably different from when NBC, CBS and ABC had the field to themselves. There is not much reason to expect that it would be different in the 500–channel era.

New technology has never lacked people to apply it. The world's presses have a capacity far greater than the number of pages they print, their output limited by the iron laws of economics, not by a shortage of writers. When the printing press made it possible to manufacture books and periodicals in great numbers, literacy spread, increasing the potential reading audience. It also unlocked the opportunity for innumerable literary talents to find expression. Within the first 50 years after Gutenberg's Bible, there were printing presses in 236 towns of Europe, a continent with 100 million mostly illiterate people that had produced some 20 million copies of between 10,000 and 15,000 different book titles, many no doubt copied from earlier manuscripts but most of them new.

The supply of would-be talent continues to exceed the demand. The number of Americans who describe themselves as authors has doubled in the last 10 years to 125,000, far more than earn their living by authorship. (In 1993, the Author's Guild, whose members write for print, had 6,500 members, and the Writer's Guild, whose members write for film and television, had 7,500. A survey of Author's Guild members a dozen years earlier found that only one-third worked at their trade full time, contributing only about one-third [at that time, $11,000] of their total family income from their writing.)

Audiences that are merely passing time do not necessarily demand much in the way of talent. Talk is cheap, and the rise of the talk show format in broadcasting and cable illustrates how easily time can be filled by the kind of empty conversation that was carried out face-to-face in the millennia before broadcasting. (Extravagant publicity on behalf of a few colorful personalities aside, talk occupies just a small proportion of listening time. It occurs mostly on AM stations, which have 30 percent of the radio audience, and only 18 percent of AM radio stations use a talk show format. Public access cable television channels, largely dedicated to talk, generate minuscule viewership.) Sure, airtime can be filled, almost *ad nauseam* as well as *ad infinitum*. But will anyone be listening?

Meanwhile, other media are not static. No mass communication medium has ever disappeared, though media have waned, changed and adapted themselves as new competitors have come along. Print media are less likely to be affected by the changes in telecommunications than is television. Text on a cathode-ray tube or liquid-crystal display simply does not communicate in the same way it does on paper, with the lure of innumerable distractions within grasp of one's fingers. Electronic tablets can supplement books and periodicals, but they cannot replace them.

Technological progress is being made in other forms of communication, not only in electronic transmission. Printing and paper-making methods are undergoing improvement, and periodical distribution systems are changing—right down to the level of the "smart" newspaper vending rack that signals home base when it is running low. Ink-jet printing makes it possible to customize publications to suit individual readers' interests. There are new ways to reassemble existing communications content and new techniques to embellish and amplify what was formerly communicated in different ways. But the essential enduring elements of mass communication remain the arts of performing drama and composing music, of observation, of collecting and interpreting information, of writing narrative.

And amidst this flood of entertainment, what happens to journalism? We turn to the news not only because its unexpected revelations may affect us directly, but because it reminds us that our world is constantly changing; it stimulates us to keep up with that change. The broadcast networks have occasionally brought live coverage of news events in the making. On cable, C-SPAN does so routinely. Interview and talk shows cast a light on the news and sometimes generate news themselves. None of these represents the kind of journalistic choices that a British newspaper reader has among the *Times*, the *Guardian*, the *Telegraph* and the *Independent* (not to mention the popular press), or that a New York reader had 50 years ago when a dozen dailies battled for circulation.

Discussion of the information aspects of telecommunications centers on the data stream, a threat to some established media, like newspaper classified advertising. The public eventually will have at its disposal an incredible reference facility made up of already existing text and visual images and a constantly revised current output. This has innumerable business and scholarly uses, but few private individuals have reason or inclination to conduct their own investigative search of secondary sources. People want information professionally picked, processed and interpreted. They want this done with an understanding of the human dramas that mere facts disguise and distort. They want it done with literary style, through the use of language that evokes imagery and emotions. That is the job of journalism. The future of journalism and of literature—like the past—largely remains with print on paper.

Communications content reflects its institutions. What is communicated cannot be separated from the mechanisms that deliver it. The rapid growth of telecommunications accompanies a decisive structural change in the way media are owned and managed. What happens to communications content depends not only on market forces; it will be determined by government actions. Regulatory rulings by the Federal Communications Commission often face years of extended litigation before they are resolved by the courts or by legislation. In the mid-1990s, two critical questions remain unresolved:

First, will a single public utility end up delivering a variety of personal and mass communication services to the households in a given geographical area, or will a number of suppliers—telephone companies, cable systems, direct satellite broadcasters, perhaps even electric power companies—be available? Mergers and other alliances between telephone companies and cable operators could create organizations so deeply entrenched and wielding such market power that the prospects for effective competition seem dim.

Second, will the same companies that control the channels through which communications reach consumers also continue to be permitted to generate communications content? The Supreme Court has upheld the right of the regional Bell companies to serve as information providers, but Congress could still separate the two functions. Cable system operators like Time Warner and Tele-Communications Inc. have used their local monopoly positions to the advantage of the cable networks in which they hold an interest by cutting off potential rivals. Is it reasonable to expect technology to find ways of leaping such formidable obstacles?

The notion of a free and open market of ideas assumes that individual media choices are unlimited. In reality, media consumers can choose only within the framework of earlier judgments made by the managements of the institutions that set the boundaries. And the public's choices are themselves determined by what is familiar, assumed to be popular and therefore acceptable.

And what will become of the audience? Conventional wisdom says that the era of the mass audience has gone forever, replaced by specialization, targeting and market niches. Yet in every type of creative endeavor, as in the marketing of consumer products, the public gravitates to the most popular offerings. A small proportion of the producers commands a very large share of total consumption. A larger array of specialized choices merely amplifies the importance of the leaders.

In spite of the growth of specialized media, monopoly reigns in most local newspaper markets. The biggest 15 percent of consumer magazines accounts for about two-thirds of all magazine circulation. Cable households can receive, on the average, 36 channels, but the four television networks still account for 62 percent of all viewing. The top-10 radio stations (out of 68) in Los Angeles have 42 percent of the total listening audience. The mass audience may have shrunk, but it has not gone away, nor is it likely to do so.

For many years, the media system has served advertisers' interests. Advertisers still pay 58 percent of the nation's mass communication budget, but their share is getting smaller and consumers are paying correspondingly more. Advertisers, who tolerate less idiosyncrasy than consumers do, tend to favor the safe middle ground. Cable television's arbitrarily designated tiers are designed to assure advertisers their audiences, but the content mix will inevitably change if selective pricing is imposed on all channels. When audiences pay separately according to the time they spend with every communication they receive, they are bound to pick and choose more carefully than when they pay a flat fee for unlimited access to an assortment of programs. (For example, when Prodigy, the leading electronic information supplier, changed from unlimited service for a set monthly fee to a charge based on actual usage on top of a modest subscription fee, its previously rapid growth stopped. Meanwhile, its flat-fee competitors flourished.) Converting all television access to a pay-as-you-go formula would reduce total television entertainment viewing hours, since a disproportionate amount of the time is spent by people who can least afford the cost. Poor people spend vastly more time than others with "free" advertiser-supported television. Time-metered service would inevitably affect the present disparities in video entertainment consumption between rich and poor.

Cable systems already pay different fees to different program suppliers, and these fees are not altogether based on audience size. The various premium services do not all charge the same rates for their films and sportscasts, and viewers have already indicated in surveys that they would be willing to pay almost twice as much for some nonpremium networks (like CNN) as for others (like the Weather Channel). If viewers paid a different price for a half-hour of access to ESPN than for the same amount of time on Arts & Entertainment, this would change the present relative size of the two audiences. The rate schedule also is likely to be different if the company that provides the distribution network has a stake in some channels but not in others.

Programming decisions made by advertisers on the basis of ratings will be modified when audiences are diminished and realigned by competitive pricing. As long as advertisers carried the cost of programming, the intensity of the viewers' motivation to watch has not been a significant factor, but it may be if pricing forces them to become more selective. If audiences are smaller, this reduces advertising cost efficiency, and in turn requires audiences to bear even more of the burden. Thus content and its consumption are shaped by the delivery system.

The American media system dedicates an inadequate proportion of its easily accessible video choices to content that enhances taste, experience, sensibility or awareness of public issues. (The $1.2 billion spent on public television, with 4 percent of the audience, and the $18 million cable industry budget for C-SPAN amount to less than 2 percent of the nation's total expenditure on broadcast and cable television. This is one-tenth of the per capita expenditure on public broadcasting in Great Britain, one-seventh of that in Japan, one-sixth of Canada's.)

Cable already offers channels devoted to science fiction, food and court proceedings. Why not repertory theater or chamber music? With an expanded array of video choices, could commercial channels catering to specialized audiences avert the need to subsidize public broadcasting? Probably not. Elite culture has never been able to rely on the market for its survival, any more than the educational system could function satisfactorily as an unsubsidized voluntary private enterprise.

What would an ideal mass communication system be like if we were inventing it from scratch? I would want it to have the following attributes:

- *Freedom.* It should permit the expression and examination of every human impulse, experience and belief without censorship.
- *Range and variety.* It should cover the spectrum of tastes and interests, with the widest possible number of choices in every sector.
- *Balance.* Amid the steady output of entertainment, it should allow information to find an appropriate place and ensure that there are multiple sources of information and opinion.
- *Innovativeness.* It should permit a constant infusion of new ideas, styles and formats (not just variations on old ideas) and give them a chance to attract a following.
- *Competitiveness.* It should be structured to encourage entrepreneurship and discourage monopoly both in delivery methods and in content.
- *Accessibility.* It should be available to all, rich and poor. (This might mean expanding the functions of public libraries.)
- *Quality.* It should be guided by standards of excellence in conception and execution, without suppressing expressions that fall short of them.

This last feature is the most likely to arouse controversy. The conventional commercial wisdom holds that standards for media content should be set by the free play of supply and demand. In practice they are, for the most part. The objection to standards of quality—other than survival or success in an open marketplace—comes from two opposite directions. On the one side is the view expressed in this book by Walter B. Wriston, who decries any value judgment on popular culture as a step toward Nazi book burning. At the other end of the spectrum is the intellectually vogue notion that standards are inherently elitist and that exquisite tastes and vulgar ones (as I would define them) are of exactly equivalent merit, since there is no anointed authority to pass judgment. I cannot agree. The issue is not one of suppressing what is bad—it is a matter of encouraging what is good.

Now who should decide what's bad and what's good?

Human behavior is often impulsive, irrational, aberrant and responsive to the immediate pressure of the moment. Standards, by contrast, require reflection. They may impose limits on behavior but they cannot dictate it. Conscience alerts us to our own improprieties; it does not prevent them. We expect to be judged and we judge others by the rules of conscience rather than by the example of our own actions. ("Do what I say," we tell children, "not what I do.") Just as people often succumb to appetites in food that conflict with what they know to be good for their health, they indulge in media tastes that are satisfying but of which they may not be proud.

It would be abhorrent to have some totalitarian or theocratic author-ity tell us that we cannot enjoy trashy magazines or movies, but most of those audiences acknowledge their trashiness, albeit with self-dis-paraging grins. People enjoy scandal and chuckle at their own frailty in enjoying it. When they think about what they want their children to like or what they would like for themselves if they had the time or the money or the energy to follow their best instincts, they distinguish between what they think is good and what they accept as pleasurable. An analogy may be seen in the difference between the snap answers people give to public opinion pollsters on serious questions and the responses they give after they have thought and talked about the sub-ject. Television programming decisions are now governed by the set-tuning records indicated by ratings. The considered judgment of our better natures deserves to be given greater weight and the producers themselves know very well what that judgment is likely to be.

The revolutionary developments under way in communications have produced an enormous amount of discussion regarding their technical, financial and legal aspects but remarkably little discussion of their social implications. The advent of television initiated studies tracing its effects on consumer markets, on other media and on individual and group behavior. From the outset, researchers compared the character-istics and actions of viewers and nonviewers and drew conclusions about the changes that television was bringing in its wake. Peculiarly, the rise of cable and of the video recorder saw no comparable effort: They were regarded as nothing more than variations of television it-self. But since advertisers demanded the information, their audiences were measured, and they turned out to be different from the former broadcast TV audience. Commercial interruptions played a different part in the pattern of viewing. The economics were different; so were the differentiation and selection of programming. Although there is ample survey evidence of the distinctions between noncable, basic cable and premium cable subscribers, there has been relatively little scrutiny of how these distinctions originate, nor have there been large-scale examinations of the differences in the nature of what is provided through different cable tiers of entertainment and information.

Research of this kind is even more needed in the present stage of transition from separate mass and personal communication systems to a single integrated system. Such research would clarify the progress of events for future historians; it would also be an invaluable guide at the present time for public policy-makers and corporate managements. It might begin with the following questions:

1. Who uses what communications channels or facilities when, why and in what combinations? (We know where.)
2. Where does the time and money come from for the new services? To what extent do they supplant existing forms of communication—electronic or print?
3. What services—packaged or available on demand—are offered and to what extent are they used? How, if at all, does the character of the packaging differ from that of comparable content in existing media?
4. How, if at all, do the new services change the use of nonmedia institutions, from the family to politics?
5. How do people differ in their receptivity to media that they must seek out and pay for, as opposed to those that are paid for by advertisers and disseminated without charge?
6. How is the use of media delimited by the mechanics of the operating devices? If the use of VCRs for recording has been curbed by their much-joked-about user-unfriendliness, how can industrial psychology be applied to solve the problems that will occur when much more complex computer control units sit on top of the display tube?

The long-term effects of the new technology must be distinguished from the flash-in-the-pan developments (like home shopping) that draw attention, encourage extravagant speculation and create instant fortunes. In 1951, when only 23 percent of the households had a television set, CBS spun its television operations off from its radio network. Key executives were given the choice of staying with radio, which accounted for almost all of the company's revenues and all the profit, or of staking their future careers in a medium that was still a novelty, off to a slow start, costly both to the public and to advertisers and losing money. In retrospect there is no question as to what was the right decision, but it was a close call at the time.

The pioneers of television had the sense that they were riding the crest of a great wave of changes that went far beyond communication to engulf every aspect of human life. They acted as self-interested business executives, but they had a keen awareness that they were leading a social revolution. The architects of today's telecommunications deals and mergers are no less conscious of the changes they are fashioning. Do they have the same sense of responsibility and concern for the consequences? If not, who will bring them to heel?

Leo Bogart, former executive vice president and general manager of the Newspaper Advertising Bureau, is author of Commercial Culture *and* Premises for Propaganda, *among other books. This chapter originally appeared in the winter 1994* Media Studies Journal, *"The Race for Content."*

23

Prospects for the Future

Compiled by Jennifer Kelley

Freedom Forum Media Studies Center dialogue and *Media Studies Journal* interviews with scholars, commentators and media professionals identified these questions for the future.

1. How will the rise of market economies and democracies shape international communications systems in the post-Cold War world?
2. Will there be a resolution to the paradox of modern media—the growth of massive global media enterprises alongside the rise of forms, such as desktop publishing, that enable individuals to produce their own media?
3. Will the rise of global media organizations and products homogenize media content and world culture? Or will the fragmentation of audience interests result in greater diversity of content and culture?
4. In the convergence of traditional news companies and telephone, cable and entertainment enterprises, which will dominate: new technologies or content?
5. Will traditional print and electronic media lose younger readers and viewers to new media?
6. Will the growth of new media compel an expansion and redefinition of First Amendment rights and a redefinition of our system of freedom of expression?
7. How will media, government and business define levels of public access to information services?
8. What will be the consequences of blurring the media functions of news and information with opinion and entertainment?
9. Will efforts to reassert the public interest through such projects as civic/public journalism succeed or fail?

10. Will hostility between industry and the academy in current debates over the training of media professionals destroy communication and journalism schools as we know them?

Prepare to Understand the Telecommunications Revolution

LEO BOGART: We usually become aware of the implications of important technological changes well after they are under way, usually after the opportunity has passed for us to reconstruct accurately what conditions were like before they occurred and began to have their effects. I fear that this is happening in the case of the telecommunications revolution.

Obviously there are all kinds of social indicators and benchmarks on what life was like in 1975 or 1980, before these new developments began to come along. But the kinds of questions we will be asking ourselves 25 years from now are not necessarily the kind that can be answered by referring to existing benchmarks. Consider what new forms of electronic communication are going to mean to the daily routine, the uses of time, the relationships of people (both within households and in larger groupings or associations formed through propinquity, work, common interests or friendship). Think of social interaction in the larger society. What is happening to the nature and location of work, the physical movement of people, to shopping and the whole retail sector of business? What are the effects going to be on the balance in the flow of information and entertainment, on the social divisions within our society?

Do we really have a body of adequate information against which to set the kinds of developments we can expect to see coming along in the next 25 or 50 years? And if we don't, and there is a gap, how can that gap be filled? How can we move now to supply the kind of information that people coming after us will want to have at their disposal when they want to look back to the origins of this change? In a parallel case, the time to have done a comprehensive national study of life before television would have been in 1946. It was only in the early '50s that we began to accumulate a body of experimental evidence comparing television and nontelevision communities, and television and nontelevision families. But by the time these studies were done, television was already an established phenomenon. There was no pretelevision benchmark to fall back on on a national scale. We are already past the point where we can do a pre-electronic information services study, and the folks in the future who will want to look back on what the effects of this have been will have to make perhaps unreliable inferences from information that is just beginning to develop.

Leo Bogart, former Media Studies Center senior fellow, is an author and the former executive vice president and general manager of the Newspaper Advertising Bureau.

Technology, Democracy and the Market

GEORGE GERBNER: The idea that technology democratizes is the typical historical fallacy that has occurred ever since electricity was first produced, and ever since the telephone and telegraph. With every one, there's basically an unthinking, uncritical view that is essentially promotional and not analytical, which says always the same thing. And it never turns out that way unless there is some democratic decision-making injected into it. There's no question that the so-called information superhighway means an increasing concentration and, through proliferation of channels, an increasing penetration into everyday life by a vastly reduced group of sources of information and entertainment. That is why every week, practically every day, there is a merger, there is a consolidation, there is a globalization; and this is positioning a handful of major players to essentially monopolize the information superhighway unless something is done. Any kind of market is essentially a plutocracy—it's run by power and it's run by money. If there is no regulation in a market to make it free, as we have done in most of our economic activities, it tends toward economic monopoly and political dictatorship.

George Gerbner is dean emeritus and professor of the Annenberg School for Communication at the University of Pennsylvania.

Whither Interactivity?

ANTHONY SMITH: Interactivity takes many forms. It can mean everything or very little, and it means that a lot of communication systems will be concerned with letting people choose material, purchase things, make acts of personal choice—whether of opinion or of purchase or of selection of material for themselves by electronic means. Now, interactivity could go a lot further and enable us to participate a lot more in the structuring of programs and in the way information sloshes about in society. Whether that really goes, whether the whole society really goes the way of e-mail and the Internet and so on is problematic, but certainly a lot more people will have the benefit of what you might call massive interactivity as opposed to minor interactivity.

And I think that a very large number of people but nothing like a majority will achieve major interactivity in the sense that they will hook up to systems that will enable them to send and receive material and that will make possible the development of media that is specially created for them—media that take on the kind of seminar role, that are neither person to person nor passive person to mass audience but something in between the two, whereby smallish groups of people can share large quantities of information and add to it as they receive it and share it with one another. In effect we would see the electronic media conduct a cultural discussion made possible by electronic means.

Another process at work is that of exactness of image through high definition television or through virtual reality because enormously enhanced processing capacity is becoming available. It means that we will, by one means or another—and there are several possible technologies—be able to have images that are a different shape and have the exactness of fine photography. Now if you merge the processes of interactivity and of exactness, or hyperimage, something very interesting will begin to happen. In terms of what most people will use these technologies for, the answer is obviously entertainment. But they will be used for commercial transactions. If you have interactive systems and high definition and moving-image high definition and the possibility of some kind of 3–D virtual-reality image, then you've really got a very valuable tool.

Anthony Smith is president of Magdalen College at Oxford University.

Who Will Pay for the Media?

LEO BOGART: The proliferation of new technology has meant that the consumer is paying an ever-increasing part of the total cost of providing the nation's entertainment and information. This has already been

dramatically visible in the case of cable; similarly the VCR has expanded the size of consumer budgets formerly spent on theatrical film-
going. Those trends are well established, but we are only now beginning to feel the impact of new on-line information services and the
evolution of CD-ROM technology.

These changes occur slowly. We are not about to wake up one
morning and find that the advertising-supported media system has
been replaced by one in which consumers are carrying all the freight,
but there is a change in the economics of media that is bound to be
reflected in its institutions and in the content of what is being provided. Some advertisers, like Edwin L. Artzt of Procter and Gamble
(the world's biggest advertiser), have expressed alarm at this development, and are concerned that the opportunity for ad-supported media
to attract large audiences may atrophy, that advertisers will no longer
have the kinds of channels to which they have become accustomed
and that attract national audiences to their selling messages. The choices
that individuals make in selecting information and entertainment are
not identical with the choices that advertisers make.

At this point one can just observe the changes taking place without
necessarily viewing them with alarm or with pleasure, but this shift in
media economics is a major development that has to be recognized
and understood. And its social policy implications have to be addressed.

An Entertainment Superhighway?

NEAL GABLER: One of my feelings about the future is that we hear so
much about the information superhighway, and I think that's really a
misnomer. I don't think it's information that's going to drive the future. Nor are people going to be driving that highway necessarily to
get information. I think what we're aiming for, and what all of the
media are converging toward, is the *entertainment* superhighway. Hard
news is an endangered species, and I think it will be extinct in the next
25 years to the point where we will not be able to recognize hard news
from soft news. The real driving force in the media is the force toward
entertainment—the force to convert everything into entertainment. And
all of these hardware mechanisms, however they seem to be evolving
now, and I'm talking about computers, cable, fiber-optics and everything else, are ultimately going to be tools—in the largest public—to

serve as vehicles for entertainment. That is not to say that there aren't going to be small groups, both outside business and within business, that are going to use these things for information purposes. When we're talking about the largest component, the most important force that the media's going to be used for over the next millennium, certainly within the next hundred years, it seems to me entertainment is going to be the key.

I think that certainly helps trivialize culture. I'm not a moralist about these things, but when everything is looked at for its entertainment value, when the news is examined for its entertainment value, when politics is essentially (though we don't call it this) analyzed for its entertainment value, when religion is examined for its entertainment value, and when entertainment, frankly, is the pre-eminent value in American life, everything tends to get trivialized. Serious issues that don't conform themselves to entertainment will not get addressed.

Neal Gabler is author of Winchell—Gossip, Power and the Culture of Celebrity *and other books on the media.*

Will Infotainment Kill Journalism?

TABITHA SOREN: You have to be more careful talking about "infotainment." It is very popular to criticize it now, but I think there are really two sides to the issue. On the one hand, I don't think the tabloid trend and "checkbook" journalism are any good. I don't think paying someone gives the interviewee any credibility. However, if President Bush or Vice President Gore goes on Letterman or Oprah or Donahue or something like that, they're going to garner an entirely new audience that they wouldn't necessarily reach otherwise. And I don't think that's a bad thing.

Tabitha Soren is an anchor and correspondent for MTV News.

New Tests for the First Amendment

JOHN CORRY: There's almost certain to be a huge proliferation of First Amendment cases. Increasingly, the courts will be called on to decide very basic questions, such as who is a journalist and what activities are protected by shield laws? For instance, if I put myself on the Internet and say I'm a journalist, does that make me a journalist? The question becomes who or what is a journalist, and I don't think that anyone has really addressed this question. But certainly we are beginning to get into these cases now, and I think we are going to get this in every federal district; every federal court in the United States is going to be handling questions like this in the years to come.

I also believe that free expression in general will come under increasing attack and that we are about to stretch the limits of the First Amendment in ways that it's never been stretched before. We may begin to find that there are some irreconcilable differences between free expression and the First Amendment. Now, in the short run, the country seems to be growing increasingly conservative on moral issues—some sort of rebellion against permissiveness and pornography and those sorts of things. I don't know how long that will last, but I suspect it's going to be around for a while.

In addition, virtual reality, it seems to me, is an utter nightmare. I don't think anyone has really thought it out yet, but its potential for coarsening the human spirit, for corrupting the human psyche is unlimited. Certainly virtual reality can be used in a number of refined, healthy, progressive ways—teaching doctors how to perform a quadruple bypass, for instance. But the great interest in virtual reality will be in sex and violence. Now I would hate to have the government control virtual reality, and I think there is simply an enormous threat there to free expression. On the other hand, I think that we will see this kind of technology under increasing attack at all levels of governments. And I certainly do not have the answer to this, but I firmly believe that we are going to see an explosion of First Amendment cases in this country that we've never encountered before. I think that there's an enormous danger in this new technology; rather than increasing our freedom, it can end up restricting it.

John Corry is "Presswatch" columnist at The American Spectator.

Journalism and Education

NEWTON N. MINOW AND CRAIG L. LAMAY: If we really want to serve our children and promote the values of citizenship and simple decency, for example, are we going to use the new technologies wisely or simply turn away? This question does not fit neatly into the marketplace mentality or into First Amendment sloganeering, but requires a kind of discussion that has yet to occur in this country. The second thing to watch for is whether educators and universities wake up to the importance of these issues. Higher education, especially, needs to take a leadership role in shaping the new communications environment. Journalism and communications schools need to rethink their role both within the academy and with respect to industry. In 10 or 15 years, for example, what will it mean to be a journalist?

Newton N. Minow, a former FCC chairman, is an attorney and director of the Annenberg Washington Program in Communications Policy Studies at Northwestern University.

Craig L. LaMay teaches at the Medill School of Journalism, Northwestern University.

The Future of Journalism and Its Public

WALTER CRONKITE: It could improve in one way: The new technology, that is, the computer and the Internet and the 500 channels and all that, can provide the inquisitive individual with more information than he or she can get today through the daily journals and broadcasts. I don't think there's any doubt about that—we'll get more information and get it faster. But on the other hand it can have the effect of even further partitioning the audience between those who are readers and intelligent viewers as opposed to those who are skimmers and don't really indulge in a thorough review of the substance.

Walter Cronkite is a CBS special correspondent and chairman of Cronkite Ward & Co.

A Need for New Voices

JANNETTE L. DATES: What I want to watch for is the trend of media research on how we have to work together as a country. The people at the top of the media are overwhelmingly white and male. They go to school together, work together, and socialize together in ways that reinforce each others' perspectives and worldviews. There's nothing wrong with being white and male, but they must open the system up so there are other representatives in the room with the power to influence decisions as decisions are made. And that doesn't mean inviting in blacks who think just like these white men. We need to hear from different voices coming from outside the dominant white male group.

Jannette L. Dates is an author and acting dean of the School of Communications at Howard University.

Learning to Cover Religion

LOREN GHIGLIONE: How will the press deal with religion and issues spiritual? I think people see it as more important than the press does. We feel uncomfortable talking about things spiritual, so we don't. However, in hiring entry-level reporters, I have noticed that young reporters of color are pleased to serve as religion editor, and they may bring a new and more sympathetic perspective to the coverage of issues of faith.

Loren Ghiglione was editor and publisher of The News *(Southbridge, Mass.) and is currently Lox Professor of Journalism at Emory University.*

Creating the Future of Journalism

SUZANNE BRAUN LEVINE: We must continue to ask ourselves what is good journalism and how it can be fostered and practiced in a changing technological environment.

Suzanne Braun Levine is editor of the Columbia Journalism Review.

In addition to those media scholars and industry leaders who are quoted in this issue, we gratefully acknowledge the following individuals, who offered their considered thoughts and helped identify the key media trends and events of the last 10 years and questions for the future: Shelby Coffey III, editor and executive vice president, *Los Angeles Times;* Frances Fitzgerald, author and journalist; Robert Haiman, president, Poynter Institute for Media Studies; Michael Janeway, dean, Medill School of Journalism, Northwestern University; Neil Postman, chair, Department of Culture and Communication, New York University; Guido Stempel III, distinguished professor, Ohio University School of Journalism.

For Further Reading

Adler, Renata. *Reckless Disregard: Westmoreland v. CBS et al., Sharon v. Time.* New York: Alfred A. Knopf, 1986.

Altschull, J. Herbert. *Agents of Power: The Role of the News Media in Human Affairs.* New York: Longman, 1984.

Auletta, Ken. *Three Blind Mice: How the TV Networks Lost Their Way.* New York: Random House, 1991.

Beniger, James R. *Control Revolution: Technological and Economic Origins of the Information Society.* Cambridge: Harvard University Press, 1986.

Carey, James. *Communication as Culture: Essays on Media and Society.* Boston: Unwin Hyman, 1988.

Clurman, Richard. *Beyond Malice: The Media's Years of Reckoning.* New Brunswick, N.J.: Transaction, 1988.

Dates, Jannette L., and William Barlow, eds. *Split Image: African Americans in the Mass Media.* Washington: Howard University Press, 1990.

Entman, Robert M. *Democracy Without Citizens: Media and the Decay of American Politics.* New York: Oxford University Press, 1989.

Frank, Reuven. *Out of Thin Air: The Brief Wonderful Life of Network News.* New York: Simon & Schuster, 1991.

Gabler, Neal. *Winchell:Gossip, Power and the Culture of Celebrity.* New York:Alfred A. Knopf, 1994.

Hallin, Daniel C. *Uncensored War: The Media and Vietnam.* New York: Oxford University Press, 1986.

Jamieson, Kathleen Hall. *Packaging the Presidency: A History and Criticism of Presidential Campaign Advertising.* New York: Oxford University Press, 1984.

Kluger, Richard. *The Paper: The Life and Death of the New York Herald Tribune.* New York: Alfred A. Knopf, 1986.

Lewis, Anthony. *Make No Law: The Sullivan Case and the First Amendment.* New York: Random House, 1991.

Lichter, S. Robert, Stanley Rotham and Linda S. Lichter. *The Media Elite.* Bethesda, Md.: Adler and Adler, 1986.

MacArthur, John R. *Second Front: Censorship and Propaganda in the Gulf War.* New York: Hill and Wang, 1992.

Manoff, Robert Karl, and Michael Schudson, eds. *Reading the News: a Pantheon Guide to Popular Culture.* New York: Pantheon Books, 1986.

McQuail, Denis. *Media Performance: Mass Communication and the Public Interest.* London: Sage, 1986.

Meyrowitz, Joshua. *No Sense of Place: The Impact of Electronic Media on Social Behavior.* New York: Oxford University Press, 1985.

Mills, Kay. *A Place in the News: From the Women's Pages to the Front Page.* New York: Columbia University Press, 1990.

Patterson, Thomas E. *Out of Order.* New York: Alfred A. Knopf, 1993.

Postman, Neil. *Amusing Ourselves to Death: Public Discourse in the Age of Show Business.* New York: Viking, 1985.

Sabato, Larry J. *Feeding Frenzy: How Attack Journalism Has Transformed American Politics.* New York: Free Press, 1991.

Schram, Martin. *The Great American Video Game: Presidential Politics in the Television Age.* New York: William Morrow, 1987.

Stephens, Mitchell. *A History of News: From the Drum to the Satellite.* New York: Viking, 1988.

Wurman, Richard Saul. *Information Anxiety.* New York: Doubleday, 1989.

Index

ABC, 97, 125–126
Abstract Expressionism, 60–61, 63
Adams, John, 151
Advertising, 85, 131, 166, 177
Akron Beacon Journal, 23–24
Alter, Jonathan, 3
American Society of Newspaper
    Editors (ASNE), 29–30
AM radio, 163
Argument, lost art of, 77–86
Arledge, Roone, 101
Armenia, 109
Arts Magazine, 61
Artworld, 59–68
Artzt, Edwin L., 177
Associated Press, 107
Atlanta Constitution, 16–17
Atlanta Journal and Constitution, 20–
    21
Audience, 166
Auletta, Ken, 72, 125–133
Author's Guild, 163

Baby Bells, 156
Bagdikian, Ben, 23, 148
Barnes, Andrew, 20
Barnett, Ross, 17
Batten, James, 30
BBC, 53, 56, 140, 145–146, 153
Bentsen, Lloyd, 100
Berlin Wall, 106
Bigelow, John, 152
Blacks: portrayal of by journalists, 23–
    31; reportage on in South, 13–21

Bogart, Leo, 152, 159–171, 174–177
Bosnia, 120
Bostock, Roy J., 130–131
Boston Globe, 45
Bottoms-up perspective, 87–94
Boylan v. Times, 33–42
The Boys on the Bus (Crouse), 43
Bradlee, Ben, 73
Branch, Taylor, 16–17
Brillo boxes (Andy Warhol), 61–62
Broadcasting Research Unit survey,
    145–146
Brokaw, Tom, 108
Brown v. Board of Education, 17–18
Bush, George, 90, 100, 109, 116–117,
    120
Bystanders, as opinion makers, 87–94

Cable TV, 6, 51–52, 156, 160, 165–167
Canada, 167
Canaday, John, 63
Cannon Group, 147
Carey, James W., 83–84
Carnegie, Andrew, 152
Carson, Johnny, 89
Carter, Hodding Jr. III, 18–19
Carter, Hodding Sr., 18
Carter, Jimmy, 53, 57, 98, 121
CBS, 97, 125–126, 170
CD-ROM, 177
Cellular phone, 114
Channel Four (Britain), 140
Chicago, Illinois, 28
Chicago Sun-Times, 25, 28

Christopher, Warren, 115, 118, 121
Chung, Connie, 100
Civil rights, 13–21
Clark, Mary Marshall, 34
Class-action suits, 35–36
Clendinen, Dudley, 13–21
Clinton, Bill, 106, 111, 119–121
CNN, 108, 116, 126–127, 136, 153
Cold War, 105–111, 119, 122
Columbia Journalism Review, 120
Commercial radio, 49–50
Communication as Culture (Carey),
     83–84
Communications Act, 50
Communications satellite, 8
Communism, end of, 105
Contras, 88
Cook, Joan, 38–40, 42
Corporation for Public Broadcasting,
     55, 57
Corry, John, 178–179
"The Cosby Show," 128
Cose, Ellis, 23–31
Cronkite, Walter, 70–72, 180
Crouse, Timothy, 43
C-SPAN, 99, 164
Cutlip, Scott, 85

Daily News, 40
Daly, Bob, 131
Damrosch, Dr. Walter, 50
Dan Burke, 125–126
"Dance in America," 54–55
Danto, Arthur C., 59–68
Dates, Jannette L., 73–74, 180–181
Davis, Horace G. "Buddy," 19
Debate, public, 77–86
Democracy, 155, 175; and public
     debate, 77–86
Democratic convention, 1988, 99–100
Demographics, 72
Dennis, Everette E., 131
Deregulation, of broadcasting, 52–53,
     139, 144
Detroit Institute of Art, 65
Dewey, John, 82–83
Dewey, Melvil, 152
Diamandis, 147
Dickie, George, 63
Digitization, 139
*Dissertation on the Canon and Feudal
     Law* (Adams), 151

Dowd, Maureen, 43–46
Dukakis, Michael, 90, 100

East Timor, 109
Educational programming, 50–54
Eisner, Michael, 131–133
Election of 1952, 96–97
Elite culture, 167
Entertainment, 160, 177–178
Entman, Robert, 28
Equal Employment Opportunity
     Commission (EEOC), 35
The Euthyphro (Plato), 64–65
Exxon, 55
Fairness Doctrine, 153

Farrell, Jack, 45
Federal Communications Commission
     (FCC), 6, 50, 165
Federal Radio Commission, 50
Film industry, 146–147
Film libraries, 162
First Amendment, 178–179
FM spectrum, 51
Ford, Gerald, 54
Foreign Affairs, 109–110
Foreign news, 105–111
Fox, 127, 130
France, 139–140
Frank, Reuven, 95–101
Franklin, Benjamin, 152, 157
Freedom Forum Media Studies Center,
     69, 131, 173
Friedman, Tom, 44
Friendly, Fred, 73

Gabler, Neal, 177
Gainesville Sun, 19
Gans, Herbert J., 48, 87–94
General Electric, 49
Georgia, 109
Georgia Gazette, 19
Gerbner, George, 175
Ghiglione, Loren, 181
Gilded Age, 79–80
The Girls in the Balcony (Robertson),
     41
Gissler, Sig, 25
Global conversation, 154
Globalization, 137–150
Glueck, Grace, 38–40, 42

"Golden Age of Television," 51
Good journalism, 3
Gore, Albert Jr., 3–4
Government subsidies, 55–58
Great Britain, 140, 167
Great Depression, 58
Greeley, Horace, 78
Greenberg, Clement, 62–65
Greene, Harold H., 153
Gresham's Law, 51–52
Grolier Company, 147
Grossman, Lawrence K., 47–58
Guardian (Britain), 164
Gulf war, 126
Gwertzman, Bernard, 108

Haber, Bill, 128
Hachette, 147
Harkey, Ira, 17–18
Harvard, John, 152
Harvard Business Review, 27
Harvey, James, 61
Harwood, John, 44
Helms, Jesse, 56
Henry, William A. III, 4
Hepburn, Audrey, 118
Herbers, John, 15
High culture, 48–58
High definition television (HDTV), 176
Hoge, James F. Jr., 105–111
Hollywood, 127–128, 160, 162
Home communication system, 161
Hoover, Herbert, 49
Horton, Willie, 90
Huger, Louise Polk, 34–35
Humanitarianism, 119
Hurok, Sol, 48
Hussein, King, 116, 153
Hussein, Saddam, 117

Image politics, 91
Independent (Britain), 164
Indianapolis Star, 25–26
Information Age, 152
Information superhighway, 159–171, 177–178
Information technology, 151–158
Infotainment, 178
Ink-jet printers, 164
Institutional Theory of Art, 60–68
Interactive media, 160, 175–176

International Herald Tribune, 136
Iowa caucus, 98
Iraq, 126

James, William, 82
Japan, 167
Johnson, Lyndon, 54
Jones, Alex, 72–73
Jones, Edward W., 27
Journalism, 164; as act of education, 3–4; and civil rights, 13–21; and education, 179–180; future of, 180–181; loss of leaders in, 73; moral condition of, 141; and its public, 70–72; role of in democracy, 82
The Journal of Philosophy, 60, 62, 65

Kalb, Bernard, 113–114
Kefauver, Estes, 98
Kelley, Jennifer, 69–74, 173–181
Kelly, Michael, 45
Kennan, George, 115–116, 118, 120–121
Kennedy, John F., 8
Korotich, Vitaly, 135–136
Kovach, Bill, 20
Kramer, Hilton, 63
Kranish, Michael, 44
Krasner, Lee, 62
Ku Klux Klan, 18
Kuralt, Charles, 49
Kurtz, Howie, 43
Kuwait, 126

The Labyrinth (Menotti), 48
Lamay, Craig L., 179–180
"Larry King Live," 153
Lasch, Christopher, 77–86
Leased telex, 113
Levine, Suzanne Braun, 181
Lewis, Tom, 155
Liberty and the News (Lippmann), 80–81
Libraries, 152
Library Company, 152
Library of Congress, 152
Licensing fees, 153
Life, 59–68
Lippmann, Walter, 80–84, 111, 143
Los Angeles, 166
Los Angeles Times, 135

Macdonald, Dwight, 51
MacNeil, Robert, 115–122
Magazines, 166
Magazine shows, 108
Mahbubani, Kishore, 109–110
Mann, Horace, 78–79
Mapplethorpe, Robert, 56, 67–68
Market economy, 140, 175
Martin, Ron, 21
Martin Marietta, 55
Mass communication system, ideal,
    167–168
Mass media, 160
Maxwell, Robert, 139
McDarrah, Fred W., 61
McGill, Ralph, 16–17, 19, 21
Media: and the artworld, 59–68; burden
    of complexes and juvenile distrac-
    tions; on, 135–136; consumer pay
    for, 176–177; future of, 173–181;
    globalism of and consumer
    sovereignty, 137–150; and race, 73–
    74; responsibility of, 3; sex-
    discrimination suits, 33–42; trends
    and events in, 69–70; truth in, 103–
    104
The Media Monopoly (Bagdikian), 23
Media Studies Journal, 69, 155, 173
Menger, Carl von, 156
Menotti, Gian Carlo, 48
Meredith, James, 17
Merz, Charles, 81
Minow, Newton N., 6–9, 179–180
Moscow coup (1991), 116
Motion Picture Association of
    America, 137–138
MTM entertainment, 147
Mugwumps, 79
Murdoch, Rupert, 138, 147–148, 153
Murphy, Tom, 125–128
Murrow, Edward, 73
Mussolini, Benito, 152
Myth, Media and the Southern Mind
    (Smith), 17

National Association of Black
    Journalists (NABJ), 26
National Endowment for the Arts, 55–
    56
National Public Radio, 57
NBC, 97–98, 125–126, 128–129

NBC symphony orchestra, 50
Networks: new economies of, 125–133;
    vulnerability of, 95–96
New Deal, 58
New Hampshire primary, 97–98
The New Republic, 81
News, 164: business of, 72–73;
    commercialization of, 71; econo-
    mies in, 130; foreign, end of
    predictability in, 105–111
Newspaper Advertising Bureau, 89
Newspaper Association of America,
    29–30
Newspaper Guild of New York, 38
Newspapers, 166; distribution system,
    141; history of, 142–143
Newsroom demographics, 29–30
Newsweek, 35–36
New York, 29
New York City, 29, 60
New York Public Library, 152
New York Times, 14–15, 28, 45, 63, 68,
    111, 135; and *Boylan v. Times*, 33–
    42
New York Tribune, 78
Nicaragua, 88
Nixon, Richard, 57
Noncommercial public broadcasting,
    53–58
North American Free Trade Agreement
    (NAFTA), 107, 110

O'Brien, Patricia, 103–104
O'Neill, Michael, 116, 154
One-sided coverage, 28–29

Packard, Vance, 85
Painting as an Art (Wollheim), 64–65
Paramount Communications, 156
Parretti, Giancarlo, 147
Parting the Waters (Branch), 16–17
Pathé Cinema, 147
Patterson, Eugene C., 16, 19–20
Pay scales, by sex, 41–42
PBS, 57, 167
The Phantom Public (Lippmann), 80–
    81
"Piss Christ" (Andres Serrano), 68
Plato, 64–65
Political conventions, 95–101
Political correctness, 29, 152

Political reporting, 43–46
Politicians, 90–91, 118
Politics, 4; public participation in, 78–79
Pollock, Jackson, 59–67
Popham, John N., 14–15, 20
Popular Culture and High Culture (Gans), 48
Portable instant voice link, 113
Portable satellite TV uplink, 113
Poynter, Nelson, 20
Printing press, 163
Print media, 79, 118–119, 164
Procter and Gamble, 177
Prodigy, 166
Programming, 167–169
Progressive Era, 80
Public access cable TV, 163
The Public and Its Problems (Dewey), 83–84
Public broadcasting, 53–58, 108
Public debate, 77–86
Public interest, 50, 52, 148
Publicity, 85–86
Public opinion, 87–94
Public Opinion (Lippmann), 80–81
Public television, 57, 167
Pulitzer, Joseph, 21
Pulitzer Prize, 18–21

Quayle, Dan, 100
Quindlen, Anna, 41

Race: issues, 13–31; and the media, 73–74
Radio, 166, 170
Raleigh News and Observer, 19
Reader's Digest, 36
Reagan, Ronald, 53, 116
Reed, Roy, 15
Regulatory systems, 141–142, 156, 165
Rehm, Diane, 155
Religion, 181
Reporters: on race, 23–31; traits of good ones, 11–12
Report of the Carnegie Commission of Educational Television, 54
The Roar of the Crowd (O'Neill), 116
Roberts, Eugene, 15
Robertson, Nan, 41
Robinson, Mary, 118

Roosevelt, Theodore, 80
Rosario v. Times, 36
Rosenblatt, Roger, 120
Rosenthal, Andrew, 45
Rush Limbaugh show, 155

St. Louis Post-Dispatch, 21
St. Petersburg Times, 20
Sarnoff, David, 49
Satellite links, 113
Scardino, Albert, 19
Schlesinger, Arthur Jr., 57–58
Schulman, Robert, 73
Seigenthaler, John, 20
Serra, Richard, 67
Serrano, Andres, 68
Sex-discrimination suits, 33–42
Shanahan, Eileen, 37
Shevardnadze, Eduard, 116
Shotzinoff, Samuel, 50
Shultz, George, 116, 153
Simpson, O.J. case, 71
Sitton, Claude, 15, 19
Skinner, Andrea, 38
Sky Television, 138
Smith, Anthony, 137–150, 175–176
Smith, Hazel Brannon, 18–19
Smith, Roberta, 68
Smith, Stephen A., 17
Socrates, 64–65
Solomon, Gerry, 130
Somalia, 109, 115–116, 118–120
Soren, Tabitha, 178
Southern newspaper editors, 13–21
Soviet Union, 105
Standards, 168
Stereotypes, 28
Stringer, Howard, 6
Subsidies, government, 55–58
Sudan, 109
Sulzberger, Arthur Hays, 111
Sulzberger, Arthur Ochs Jr., 41–42
"Summertime" (Jackson Pollock), 62
Sun (Britain), 145
"Sunday Morning," 49
Supreme Court, 165
Symbolic politics, 91

Tajikistan, 109
Talk shows, 163
Taylor, Billy, 49

Technology, 113–114, 119, 121–122, 132–133, 139–140, 153–156, 164, 175–176
Telecommunications, 6, 160–171; revolution in, 174–175
Tele-Communications Inc., 165
Telegraph (Britain), 164
Telephone, 160
Television, 154–155, 164, 169; affect on foreign policy, 115–122; commercial vs. high culture, 48–58; destabilizing influence of, 70–71; marketplace, 7; pioneers of, 170–171; as "vast wasteland," 5–9
Television Without Frontiers (European Community Green Paper), 137
The Tennessean, 20
Thatcher, Margaret, 56
Theobald, Bill, 25–26
Tillim, Sidney, 61
"Tilted Arc" (Richard Serra), 67
Time, 108
Times (Britain), 145, 164
Times-Picayune, 25
Time-Warner, 147–148, 165
Tisch, Larry, 125–129, 132
Title VII class-action cases, 35–36
Tocqueville, Alexis de, 6, 155
"Today," 127
Today (Britain), 145
Top-down perspective, 92
Toscanini, Arturo, 50
Town meetings, 79
The Transfiguration of the Common-place (Danto), 63
Transnational media, 143–149
Truman, Harry, 14–15, 17

20th Century Fox, 147

UHF channels, 51
United Artists, 147
United Nations, 119
United States, 142
USA Today, 21, 135

VCR, 6, 160, 177
Videotape, 113
Virtual reality, 176
Wade, Betsy, 33–42

Wall Street Journal, 135
Warhol, Andy, 61–62
Washington Post, 135
Washington Press Club Foundation, 34
Wealth creation, 157
Welch, Jack, 126–127, 129–130
White, E.B., 8
Whitney Museum, 67–68
Wines, Michael, 44
Winship, Thomas, 11–12
Wire services, 138
Wisconsin primary, 97–98
Wolfe, Tom, 48
Wollheim, Richard, 64–65
World War II, 70
Wright, Bob, 125–127
Wriston, Walter B., 151–158, 168
Writer's Guild, 163

Yeltsin, Boris, 116
Yugoslavia, 109

Zuckerman, Eugenia, 48